# Christianity

# at a

# Crossroads

Timothy Thomas

Published By Torah for Gentiles

Check us out online at

www.torahforgentiles.webs.com

For Additional copies go to

www.torahforgentiles.com or

http://www.amazon.com

ISBN 9780992085704

Printed in the United States

# Dedication

I want to thank my amazing wife Hazel for putting up
with me, and wonderful daughter Kathleen for constant
inspiration, and her amazing squinches, you guys are my joy
and life, without which I would be lost. I love you guys. I also
want to thank Dennis, Lynzie, Lin, and everyone else who
helped me finish this project.

# Table of Contents

Introduction                                                    5

Chapter 1 Who Is The Church?                                   10

Chapter 2 The Churches Cynicism for the Truth                 25

Chapter 3 Does the Church have a Problem?                     52

Chapter 4 Is Peter the Head of the Church?                    67

Chapter 5 Were the Apostles Rabbis or Philosophers?          99

Chapter 6 Was the Church meant to be a Kingdom?             114

Chapter 7 Was Origen a friend or a foe?                     136

Chapter 8 Is Scripture Hebrew or Greek?                     156

Chapter 9 Where are the Original Copies?                    162

Chapter 10 Should we look like a Greek or Hebrew?           178

Chapter 11 Early Church Fathers Teachings                   194

Chapter 12 What is Torah Study?                             211

# Introduction

Our Societal morals, boundaries, and rules are changing dramatically. This is not new. Peoples of different generations and countries have gone through these changes before, and if the Lord tarries will continue to go through them. I believe that we as a believing society have a responsibility to not only meet these changes head on, but also choose the proper path, before one is chosen for us again, as it was in the Third Century. This book is about knowing why you believe what you believe. Don't leave societal changes to others, become a part of the changes.

There is a conundrum to being human, we are all connected innately to and by God, but we also make up our own hearts whether we follow Him or not, he only shows us the path, or contends with us to follow, we say yes or no. Do not let your yes be a no, or your no a yes because society has moved so far from what you are accustomed to. Realize what truth is, and then make the proper decision to follow or not.

What I have tried to do in this book is to crystallize one of my main bones of contention with how the behemoth structure called the Church has tried to make it almost impossible for simple minded people to just live and believe. The church structure is a top down structure rather than a bottom up structure. This ideology needs to be looked at because Jesus clearly taught the Church should have a bottom up look, rather than top down.

I read a legend about the Apostle John which came to us through possible wrong channels but has a very good message. The legend confirms that the Apostle John had been sent from Ephesus his home to the Island of Patmos by the Emperor Domitian. He lived in a small cave with one other person, some say it was a very young Polycarp, who helped him with his daily needs because he was old and Patmos was a very difficult place to live, there were no McDonalds, or even Inns there, you were on your own to get by however you could.

The Emperor who sentenced him there had been killed in 96 AD, and with his death the decree was forgotten so he could go home to Ephesus and live out his days in peace with people who loved him. When he went back to Ephesus, as the legend goes, he joined all the believers for the Sabbath. They still celebrated the

Sabbath. Constantine hadn't changed the services yet. By this time he was old and had to be carried on a mat by the young men.

The young men would carry him to the place where they all gathered together and set him down hoping he would regale them with stories of their Lord. Instead every Sabbath he would look at the men and the women and simply say the phrase "Little Children, love one another."

The people continually waited for him to tell them how they could love one another, why they needed to love one another, but no other sayings came. Each time they saw the Apostle he would recite these words "Little Children love one another."

Finally the people of the Church were wearied to the point of frustration and asked their beloved Apostle, "Master, you always only tell us to Love one another, why?"

The Apostle then looked each person in their eye and said with all the power of the Holy Spirit, "It is the Lords Command, and if you only do this it will be enough." After he said this it is reported he passed in his sleep, with a smile on his face.

This is something we as the Church needs to remember, love one another. To love one another as the Lord wants, we need to know what we believe and why we believe it, not get lost with societal pressures. The love the Apostle John was talking about was not the type of love we experience today when we become part of the church I assure you. It also seems that it is not something we are the only ones struggle with. If this legend is true then we can see the First Century Church struggled with the same things. In John's letters he stressed this as well.

This book has sprung from my own study of why the church thinks the way it does, and how that thinking allows the church to forsake the love it is called to do because of the conclusions of their linear thinking. To truly love one another is to think properly, and think properly is to know why you think the way you do.

# Chapter 1

## Who Is The Church?

There is an old idiom Evangelists use when they are asked why they feel the need to preach the Gospel so strongly. I have heard this phrase from people as diverse as Mother Teresa, to Ray Comfort, to a mentor of mine named Danny Lehmann, they say from their hearts

"I feel like I am a beggar who has found some bread, and I want to help other beggars find bread for themselves."

I echo this sentiment, I feel all of us humans are here on this planet not of our own choosing; we were created by God, and sent here with a purpose. Sometimes, our purpose in life makes us into an anonymous part of the overall fabric of society; sometimes it means we are to be leaders, and other times just become part of a group of believers. Who we are our stations in life are not our purpose.

Every person on the planet has a real purpose, and we all, no matter what station we live in, have the same purpose, this purpose is what binds us as one. Our purpose is simply to follow and worship the Creator who placed us here. This is not a difficult task because it is innate in ALL humans who are alive. Our purpose is one which dominates all the others and puts into context why we as humans are all alike, no matter our station, culture, or place in life. This purpose is right in everyone's heart; no one can escape it.

Without the dynamic of having to choose to worship and follow God, or not worship and follow Him we would not be tied together, nor would a Creator even exist, but because we are tied together through this struggle in our hearts and minds. We know that no matter what country we are from, what language we speak, our hearts were made by the same Creator.

You may think my view is simplistic, but look at what Genesis 6:3 says, *"Then the LORD said, "My Spirit will not contend with humans forever, for they are mortal; their days will be a hundred and twenty years."*

This for me is important to understand, because it shows many things, but most importantly we see that God is in charge of life. We also see through this that God has a relationship with all Humans. He also controls this relationship, and we are all bound to this relationship with Him.

This is a very simple Scripture but one that is powerful for all of mankind to understand. Not only does it connect us to the same source of life, but it puts us on the same playing field of relationship status with the Creator. No one has more access, or less access to God, we are all equal because God's Spirit contends with us equally.

Let us look at what Jesus' desire for His Disciples? He said this to his Disciples,

John 15:14-17, *"14 **You** are my friends **if you do** whatever I command you. 15 **No longer do I call you servants**, for a servant does not know what his Master is doing; but **I have called you Friends**, for all things I have heard from My Father I have made known to you.16 **You did not choose Me, but I chose you and appointed you that you should go and bear fruit, and that your fruit should remain, that whatever you ask in My Name He may give it to you.** 17 These things I command you, that you love one another."*

Here are some ways the Church uses to view this Scripture.

1. This was **only** meant for the Disciples who would become the Apostles of the Church; the Churches who teach this are now becoming extinct.

2. This blessing was meant for the original hearers, and all the succeeding generations of Disciples who would come after the original hearers thus making all of us Jesus' personal friends, and not only servants.

3. This was an allegory on how to properly be a friend of God and man; the Churches who teach this also teach that this introduced the concept of clergy laity.

4. This is a farewell address that Jesus gave to His Disciples stressing in an allegorical way the importance of His Words thus making His Words able to be used as metaphors for understanding the Nature of God.

This particular saying of Jesus has been looked at through all of the ways I cited above, and unfortunately some of the conclusions these thoughts produce negate the Old Testament's validity.

When I look at this passage I have these questions.

1.  How did Jesus actually want these words to be seen? Was he really trying to setting up a hierarchy with them, or maybe not setting it up just defining it in a metaphorical way? I.E. Obey Commands=Friend, Friend= Secret Status, Servant=Bad, Chosen=No Personal Choice, If you Bear Fruit=Blessed by God, Fruit=Obeying Jesus' Commands. Is this the type of message He was sending?

2.  How does a 20<sup>th</sup> Century man or woman, define biblical love, which is in step with Jesus' understanding given here? What does it mean to love the Lord without the Torah or the Law (meaning here the ethical system of belief contained in the first five books of the Bible)? How can we say the Torah has been done away with when Jesus clearly says here that we need to use Love to follow Him, which He never defined in His Sayings? Paul defined love, but Jesus only makes commands not explanations of how to understand the commands. How can we as 20<sup>th</sup> Century non-Jews understand His meaning of terms like Love, Fruit, and Servant without understanding how He would have understood these terms.

3. If this saying was for everyone, did Jesus just assume every culture, every age, and every person who read His Words, would understand the meaning of Love, Fellowship, and Community building concepts He is giving us here? When Jesus explained this did he assume everyone would naturally know what doing His commands meant, or understand the concepts here just by the etymology of the words spoken, or did He hope the Torah Principles in His hearers life would explain the terms he was telling His Disciples to do?

4. Was Jesus trying to start a New Nation with these Words, realizing the Twelve Tribes of Israel had failed? In Jesus' mind was not being a servant equal to a New Nation of Gods Elect? Was Jesus' negating the Jewish Nation here and setting up an whole new Nation?

5. Did Jesus believe somehow, the twelve Jewish men who He called to be His Emissaries or Apostles would finally be able to organize a mass of humanity to embody these truths? Is this passage confirmation that Jesus was setting aside Israel and setting up a new Authority structure for His People?

6. Did Jesus believe that His Commands were new teachings, which alone could teach people to properly love each other because of the inherent power of the words? Was Jesus confident that His Words and His Words alone taught people how to Love properly, or was He coupling these Words with the foundations already laid in the life of His Disciples by the Torah understanding of love, servant, and fruit bearing?

I ask these questions because this passage can go many different ways. I used to think, keep it simple; if you ask too many questions you will get off track or get lost in the minutia of the details rather than the principle. I have found as I walk with the Lord that the details I was afraid to look into are very important to understand.

Many of the Churches answers to these questions have either no empirical basis in Scripture, are only a guess, or are from the 3rd Century leaders which came up with a logical construct from the Greek Language which had no basis in Scripture.

As an example I will cite the churches belief that it is a Kingdom, this is nowhere in Scripture. Jesus never said He was setting up a Kingdom, he actually said, *John 18:36, 36 Jesus said, "My kingdom is not of this world. If it were, my servants would fight to prevent my arrest by the Jewish leaders. But now my kingdom is from another place."* This was spoken to a direct question Jesus received from Pontius Pilate about being a King and in charge of Kingdom. I do not believe Jesus was nervous about saying he was setting up a Kingdom, but He emphatically denied setting up an Earthly Kingdom.

There are so many other teachings, some of my favorites are that the Church believes there is a clergy and laity. This is also nowhere in Scripture unless you adopt a Greek way of thinking about the Words of Jesus and the Apostles. There is also nothing in Scripture which says the Twelve Tribes have been replaced by the church or by men and women who believe that Jesus is God.

Most of these doctrines are skin deep with respect to a Scriptural basis, but because Pastors have been teaching these doctrines for Centuries, we as believers have no choice but to accept them. At first I chose to trust and obey, because the change Jesus wrought in my life had been permanent and inescapable. It also seemed to be the same experience the majority of the people in Church had.

I continued to study and attend Church and tried very hard to ignore things I knew were unscriptural, and was amazed to find, before the Third Century and advent of Church Councils the Church leaders studied something I had never heard of before, the Torah.

At the time I didn't realize it was the Torah they studied, this knowledge would come later. As I studied these men's words, I saw men who followed from their hearts, but had a solid basis for what they believed. These teachings were simple and straightforward and did not spring from Platonic influences.

It had a basis in fundamental simple biblical logic, and made these men into people who could endure every hardship as a good soldier of Christ. These men gave me hope there was good teachings out there to study.

I need to explain why it matters to discuss these issues. In the coming years we will see that **how** we study, will be just as important as what we study. For the past 1,500 years or so the Church has been using a Platonic way to interpret the Scriptures, holding firm to this dialectical approach on interpreting what scripture means. Since the time of 325 AD the Church has used a Greek linear approach, as well as a Platonic model of philosophy to interpret Scripture, which differs greatly from how the Apostles and Jesus would have interpreted Scripture.

For clarification, I believe the Church is defined by people who have given their hearts and souls to the Lord as Romans 10:9+10 says, there are no hidden super believers. I do not believe that people have any special or hidden knowledge, the Church are those of us who claim Jesus as our Savior and Lord, and we are all in this together whether we realize it or not.

The Church is not the people or the different Denominations. The Church is the people who believe in Jesus as Messiah. What is important in the coming years is for us as a Body of Believers to get our heads screwed on right about how we think and study.

How the World understands right from wrong is dramatically changing. Our Holy Scriptures will not be used in the proper way when it comes to following truth, but will be twisted in ways we cannot even fathom right now.

Up until this present age of "knowledge at your fingertips", and integration of cultures, our basic societal dialectical approach stayed the same. Now we need to be careful because the societal dialectic is becoming a hybrid of vastly different religious cultures and beliefs, this makes the lines of truth blurry at best, and wrong at worst.

In every age there are differences, but are age is one of the first to experience Buddhism, Islam, Judaism, and Christianity all mixed into one culture. There are naturally going to be blurry lines of societal truth because of this. We do not now have the basic Judeo-Christian underpinnings we were used to.

We will see in the coming years that people we trusted to teach us proper doctrine will begin to change their opinion because of social pressures rather than truth, and no matter how deep and heart-felt understandings we have, they will begin to try and teach us that the old way was wrong and the new way will lead us into the life we desire.

There are many reasons for this change, but one of the main reasons I believe the Western Worldview is changing, is because of the way the church began interpreting Scripture 1500 years ago. Please do not misunderstand me, the Lord has allowed the Plato inspired dialectic to continue, and He has also allowed Church movements to be formed and prosper by using this type of logic of Scripture.

I do not think the elitism which began with the first leaders of the Roman Churches 1500 years ago was blessed by God but it became the way of "doing business" and stuck until today, but the organizational model adapted for the Church 1500 years ago by these Elitist's has stood the test of time, which means that the Lord has chosen to use this model until now to spread His message.

No matter what we believe Scripture means, the Lord will weed out the things which are against him, and He has done this continually throughout the 2000 years of the Church. What He does mainly and continually is to accept anyone whose heart is pure, even if the doctrine accepted may not be the most accurate.

In my opinion God is concerned with people not doctrines, if He was concerned about doctrines then He would have made robots, but He didn't. He made us with imagination, a propensity to love; we can change our behaviors which can then lead to social and health changes in our bodies, we also desire to understand the Creation down to the basic building block. This was all given to us by the Creator so we could not be robots, but a race with free will, able to choose honestly to follow or not follow.

At this time of social change, we need to realize that up is down, and down is up with respect to what were formerly Judeo-Christian values like family and marriage. The things which may appear to be right socially may be wrong biblically.

Now, instead of family being the center of the culture in the West, money making and convenience seems to be. When a person then is family centered they are considered odd and not up on the times.

In today's world instead of following a set of ethical rules for life, it seems that entertainment has taken this part of Society, and teaches people its brand of ethics and worldview.

Instead of looking to the future and bettering your children's lot in life, today's people look to spend everything on the present and only think of today and ourselves. Change comes to many cultures, we need to realize it and become centered in what the Lord wants for us not society.

In the past 20 years the church intelligentsia, which in my mind is the Theologians who write the doctrines of the churches, are changing. A new type of Scholar is emerging with respect to Christian Theology. These people are not like the early 1900 scholars. Men like Dietrich Bonheoffer, Louis Berkhof, Karl Barth, Christian Weisse, Soren Kierkegaard, or the Niebuhr Brothers.

The former Theologians mainly interpret the Scriptures in a linear Platonic way. This was started in my opinion when Constantine made Christianity the main Religion of Rome. They never questioned this type of thinking but instead just thought in a linear way and thus wrote down their ideas through only this type of thinking.

The Scholars of today's Seminaries are grappling with a very difficult topic, and this centers on how Christians should think about Scripture, should we go with the age old Platonic way, or the older Rabbinic or Judaic Interpretive models, or try to make a hybrid approach of the two.

This would at first glance seem to not interest a non-scholar, but I am here to say that it should not be a discussion we as believers leave to an elite group of men who may or may not be picked by the Lord to decide how we study the Scriptures. We should all become acquainted with these discussions, and educate ourselves on why we think the way we do.

Throughout history of thought, there have always been the haves and the have not's, usually the have not's become the villain and are not heard from again. They usually do not have a say in future generations understanding of belief, life, or Nation building. Mostly, the losers of any battle do not stay around much for history to record their valid arguments.

In the First Century church there were two models of interpretive method. One came from the Pharisaical Sects started by Ezra, and the other came from the third generation of believers, started mainly with non-Jewish Hellenistic believers. Some say that Paul was a Hellenistic minded Jewish man, which means he accepted the Greek way of life instead of living as a Hebrew. I disagree with this commonly held position and will explain why when we delve into how the Apostles thought. In the next chapter I will explain why I personally care about this stuff.

---

# Chapter 2

## The Churches Cynicism for the Truth

When I first became a believer I excitedly told my family I was called to be a missionary and was going into a Mission organization called Youth with a Mission or YWAM. My mother was an unbeliever and hated my decision to go into this organization, we argued vehemently about my desire to serve the Lord. She wanted me to not attend church or at least only attend the Catholic Church.

My father was called into Missions when he was young, his family attended a Baptist church and he was one of the most devout in the church according to my Aunts and Uncles. When they spoke of him they referred to his call with reverence and huge disappointment.

Before he went to Bible College he decided to go into the Army. When he returned from his Army service in 1960 his only belief seemed to be drinking himself into stupor when not working, watching sports, or pornography.

He had lost his relationship with the Lord and instead accepted another more damaging worldview of entertainment, sedating himself with alcohol from the truths he knew. I believe he misused alcohol because he knew that the Bible was true, but felt he wasn't good enough to follow its precepts.

When I was 12, I found a Bible that was given to him by one of his uncles who was a Pastor. It was a King James Version of the Thompson Chain Reference Study Bible. When I read it, I didn't comprehend anything but loved the stories in Genesis and Exodus. My dad never said anything when he saw me reading the Bible. Then at 18 after a very eventful time of disobedience the Lord called me out of darkness and into His Light, from then on my life has had purpose and meaning.

I thought my parents would be excited about my being called into Missions, but when I told them I was going to another country I was shocked at my mom's immediate violent reaction. This was one of the few times after I left home that both of my parents tried to tell me not to do something I knew I was supposed to do. My mom was violently opposed to me joining some Christian group in Hawaii she felt was a cult, as all non-Catholic groups were in her mind. My dad tried to explain to me that I should see the reaction I caused my mother was a warning.

He explained to me that he also was supposed to go into Missions and was glad he didn't because it was something which tears families apart. He never explained what this meant, but I found out later he was speaking about how his parents, friends, and people he respected told him that if he married my mom they would have to disown him because he couldn't fulfill his destiny married to an unbeliever. In his mind his 'Call' into Missions caused his family to reject my mother.

When he told me his feeling about giving all to serve the Lord, I remember being filled with indignation and simply told him,

"When I get to be your age I want to be a Godly man who knows right from wrong and not waste my life on negative things." he was 54 at the time, "God in our lives do not hurt families, its rejection of Him which hurt families."

He looked at me sadly and then went back to his beer and never told me anything else about my Christianity until his death bed, but that's a story for another book.

I share that story because I gave up my family's blessing to do what I knew the Lord wanted me to do. When I made it to YWAM (Youth with a Mission), I found the people were excited about the Lord, and more importantly about serving Him.

Most had amazing families who supported their decision and saw the good in what they were doing. What my father said to me about serving the Lord proved to be wrong. There were no broken up families, instead there was love, grace, and humility, and the problems which arose were dealt with in a biblical way, and led to reconciliation and increased belief.

The people I was around were also not professional, but people, who chose to believe in prayer, chose to worship, and most of all, chose to follow Jesus with their whole heart no matter the problems or joys in their lives. They all chose to innocently believe and trust. There were problems of course; no place on Earth is perfect but it was a good place with good people.

What I experienced in YWAM was what can happen when a group of believers decide to innocently follow the Lord in their hearts. The time of Discipleship and preparation I had in YWAM, made me realize we need like-minded people to encourage us to serve the Lord, because ultimately we are all weak and prone to follow our own destructive desires. When there is a community which prays, seeks, and worships the Lord the ups and downs of life are easier to deal with. I felt Bible College would be similar to the experience I had at YWAM, but I was wrong.

When I entered Bible College it was with the same type of enthusiasm of wanting to learn, grow, and become better equipped for service I had when entering YWAM. I felt the Lord wanted me to go to the School I enrolled in, I was accepted which was good. A very good friend of mine who had the same type of heart for belief enrolled with me so he could finish his biblical degree he had started years before. I was with friends and excited to learn.

As I encountered the different classes, students, and professors, I found that Jesus didn't consume the people as much as He did with me and my friend. There were a small minority in the school who had the same beliefs as I had in respect to whole-hearted devotion, but the innocent naiveté about the scriptures and simple belief and trust in the Lord were not most of the student's background.

Most of the students in the school, which ranged in age from 18-45, were concerned with things not on my radar. The students were concerned about things like making money, becoming a Christian celebrity, careers, or starting families. These are not bad things, in and of themselves but they were things I was not in Bible College for, I was there to learn.

As I continued attending and seeing how things were in the school. I tried to understand why people's concepts seemed to center on worldly things, rather than prayer and whole-hearted devotion. I tried to believe that my fellow students were not being rebellious but only doing what their leaders had taught them to do. In YWAM, Discipleship was never pretty, but it was always effective. What I was seeing in the school was a serious lack of discipleship. This made me wonder why.

I have always asked the why questions, it is who I am. I asked many why questions there because I was being confronted with people who said they honestly wanted to go into the Ministry to help others see the Lord, but then on the weekends would party like unbelievers. This did not compute to me. I came out of that lifestyle and knew a disciplined life of prayer and devotion fully met the needs of wanting to party.

One of the big why questions was about the Professors, I asked why they put up with the attitudes, and behavior of the students. I watched the Professors advice and behavior towards the students, and would sit and ask questions of all the Professors to see how they dealt with the students.

I can understand bit of rebellion in people who are just becoming disciples, but the professors seemed to share the student's cynicism over innocently following the Lord. I realize that we as humans have been rationalizing sin since Adam was kicked out of the garden, but what I saw from the Professors was a move toward blatant rewriting of history, and what biblical texts mean in order to allow them to live as an unbeliever.

The Bible College I went to was small, everyone knew each other; we also worked with many of the Churches in the area, and the Pastors trusted the different Professors almost too much. At this time there was a focus on reintroducing the Gospel in a context where people who never went to church would feel comfortable in church. Churches like Willow Creek, and Saddleback were just becoming popular styles to emulate.

I saw many of the professors as perfect representatives of church doctrine on Sunday, but when it came to the week in their classrooms they tried desperately to come as close to the worlds philosophies as they could without losing their jobs.

The biblical topics the Professors were teaching were standard bible college fare, but the Professors cast a cynical eye toward the age-old truths, which by osmosis made the students become cynical as well. They wouldn't announce their skepticism publicly of course, but when I would question them alone, or bring up questions in the class they all seemed to not believe what they taught, or to not even have researched the material before teaching it.

Some of the Professors had taught the same subject for years on end, so familiarity with the material should not have been an issue; it seemed to me and my friend, that the issue was more a lack of enthusiasm for the subject matter. Most professors told us privately their belief that everyone needed to get through what, they said, was the first stage of leadership training, Bible College. They explained that after we finish this stage we would have the credibility to be able to set up whatever ministry we wanted. In their minds whatever the student personally believed had no relevance to the chosen profession of being a Christian Pastor. They explained their job was to show us how to become a professional in the church, then we could help in whatever way we deemed necessary. I found this mindset of building professionals to be nauseating.

One Professor in particular was fired because he believed in Evolution, much to the dismay of my own Pastor who thought he was a close friend and colleague of this man, only to realize that this man was hiding his true beliefs on Genesis. Out of all the Professors in the school this man was the one who was most honest and forthright with what he believed.

He didn't have an underhanded conspiracy to infiltrate the Bible College and enlighten the students, but instead, he believed he came to a different conclusion of belief in respect to how the World was made, and for him it was all academic and proper within the philosophy of the Christian Church. I spent many hours discussing with him why he believed Evolution was a true theory; He believed he was well within his rights to believe this theory about beginnings because the core sciences of the World were in favor of it rather than Creation. The tenets of the Bible College stated however that it believed in a literal 7 day Creation process, so once he was known as a man who did not believe their doctrines he had to leave the school.

The other Professors for the most part had similar questions of belief but never would have been as blatant with their questions as this man, and because of this they were able to keep their jobs. What I learned from being around these men, was that they believed in Christianity, and wanted to have a deep personal relationship with the Lord, but because they were 'professionals' they had to keep their heart beliefs and questions quiet in order to toe the line. I found the culture of this somehow to be wrong.

Then I had a class called Biblical Exegesis, in it we learned how to tear apart a biblical passage by its original language, context, and historical meaning. There were 2 verses we had to choose from to exegete for our final project. One was a New Testament verse out of Romans, and the other one was an Old Testament verse called the Shema by the Jews. I chose the Old Testament verse because I always loved the Jewish people and wanted to learn more about this verse. As I dug into it I was pushed into a world I didn't know existed.

I had to research the verse through mostly Jewish sources as the Christian sources had very little to say about the root Hebrew meanings of the verse. In Biblical Exegesis the main idea is to take the bible verse and see what it means regardless of traditional belief and understanding. It is to get to the root meaning, the real truth of the verse. I loved the idea; it was in line with how I thought.

As I tore apart the verse for the project, I found that the Jewish sources were amazing. They knew everything we Christians knew, only they knew for a thousand years before

Jesus came. I was astounded by their depth of devotion, belief, and understanding. I was also amazed that for every question they had a reasonable answer. I will explain this in more detail in chapter eight.

Most Christian Theology books only bring up more questions, rather than answers. The Jewish writings however had concrete, biblical, and reasonable answers to the most difficult ethical questions I had. I became hooked on Jewish wisdom writings after this class.

I started the fourth semester of my Bible College career and immersed myself in Judaic writings. My friend who enrolled with me and another person we had become close to also were attracted to this whole world of Judaic thought and practice.

We started celebrating Sabbath together as the First Century Church had done; we also studied these amazing books of wisdom we had found in whatever spare time we had, and we all realized we found something we had always been looking for.

I was getting good grades at school, and wasn't concerned so much about why the people in the school were not like me, or why I wasn't like them anymore. I was learning, growing, and worshipping the Lord in a very powerful way. The one thing in that time of growth I was certain of however was I didn't believe Christian Theology's ways on how to study the scriptures.

I realized I was reduced to three main beliefs in life;

1. I knew Jesus had completely changed my life and without Him I was nothing, I was not Jewish nor did I want to be

2. I believed that people who knew Jesus were brothers and sisters no matter their Theology

3. I had found the answers to some of my theological questions through Jewish Wisdom Writings

Beyond this, I did not know where to look to find a group of like-minded believers, how to go about incorporating this new belief system into my life without rejecting my Christian friends who didn't want anything to do with the Jews, and cast me out of their world because of my enthusiasm for sharing what I was learning in the Jewish writings I was reading.

It hurt me to lose friendships I had developed over years of service to the Lord, but the Lord was so close to me in this time I endured the rejection much easier than I would have been able to before I found a prism of Judaic understanding to look through.

I remember I was in Chapel in the middle of my fifth semester, and felt the Lord move in my heart that I needed to move to Southern Missouri to be with my parents who I hadn't lived with for over 17 years. I was 30 and had left home at 15. I was very excited as I told my friends the Lord had released me from Bible College, but wondered why the Lord would send me to Missouri.

One thing I never questioned then or now, was the Lords direction, whether it is through prayer or circumstances, after I know where the Lord is leading, it is difficult for me to not go in that direction.

I knew I needed a degree but figured I could finish at some other college, and wanted to follow the direction I felt the Lord was moving me in. I will always be thankful for the year I had with my dad, it was difficult, but also a chapter I needed to write within the novel of my own life. My father passed away almost 1 year to the day I moved to Missouri.

My experience in Bible College was something which I have discussed with many people who have went to other schools; and most say that they had similar experiences in respect to seeing the professor's attitudes. The only difference in my friends is they never asked why the professors have this attitude. They either ignored the questions, or accepted the attitudes of the professor's and then adopted them in order to fit in themselves.

I have also become friends with some people who not only understand where the professor's attitudes come from, but also believe it is the proper path for the church to have. Their reasoning runs the gamut from accepting that we all believe what we believe after accepting the truth; to no one believes everything right anyway, to the final belief of toeing the Theological lines and keep our questions to our own times with the Lord.

I had spent around 15 years in Missions and then Bible College, but had been reduced to believing that somehow the Christian church had accepted a belief system I could not. It left me as a bit of an outsider in a world I felt I belonged in, that being the world of Christianity, specifically Missions.

My friends and I did turn to other groups of people who were having the same crisis of believing Greek minded Christian doctrine. We attended Messianic conferences, we listened to ethical teachings from various Rabbis, and one of my friends even came close to converting to Judaism to block out the difficulty of realizing we do not believe in the fundamental Greek way of interpreting Scripture as most of our fellow believers do. After going down these different paths that were dead ends, I decided to wait on the Lord to reveal to me what this upheaval all meant.

I ended up meeting and marrying my beautiful bride which forced my brain to set aside its questions of why, in order to raise our daughter, and get used to living with someone who has estrogen rather than testosterone. Marriage and parenthood is an amazing journey of discovery in and of itself.

I would not say that I understand the complexities of how males and females coexist in the bonds of matrimony fully yet, but my wife has graciously allowed me to resume my why questions. I am now pursuing why I believe different than most Believers.

---

Marriage is something that has helped me see the layers of how we build a belief system, which is one of the main reasons I think this discussion is very important to have right now.

I have realized one of the main reasons I am disenchanted with church theology is because I believe we are at the end of the age of Greek thinking for the Church. With the Nation of Israel now a reality, and the Roman Catholic Church losing its grip on World power, other cultures are taking hold. The Greek mindset set up by men like Plato, Socrates, Constantine, Augustus, and Thomas Aquinas seem to becoming obsolete, this affects Christians dramatically because our culture has changed now and we are alone in our beliefs about God.

What is emerging is a joining of many cultures and the diminishing of other cultures. In my opinion, Greek culture specifically democracy, is being minimized now, and older systems of thought like Judaic is coming to the forefront for religious minded people because of its veracity, and its ability to explain how to reconcile faith, with emerging beliefs entering our world by what is called science.

The Greek mentality allows scientific theory to infiltrate it and change its core philosophy of belief. This to me is untenable. What I mean is that if the Church will allow the supposed breakthroughs of science to change age-old beliefs about Creation, family relationships, and social responsibilities our beliefs are pop culture, not something that we can build lives on.

If the philosophical approach of core belief can be undermined by pop culture or new theories, I cannot endorse this type of philosophy as valid, because then the absolute truth within it isn't about belief but ethical laws alone. This is nowhere more evident than in the case of abortion and homosexual marriage. The Bible speaks about absolute truths, not just ethical laws. The ethical laws are meaningless without the core belief understood. In my opinion, I believe we need to teach our children and ourselves that Biblical Ethics are not sliding scales, if you believe then sin has to be explained properly from the Bible not cultural norms.

Evolutionists would say this is to be brain-washed but they miss a key point. They assign a philosophy (Evolution) to empirical evidence which could not be understood without a theory of belief.

To say certain rocks, fossils, or ages of the Earth are billions of years old because of your philosophy says that they are, is just as silly as saying the World was created in 7 literal days. No one has been around for billions of years, there has never been any lab able to prove that anything can change genus after thousands or millions of generations of life, and the mathematicians odds for Evolution to have been a way of how the World are so great it is impossible unless you believe in the theory of evolution.

Whenever I talk with a real Evolutionist I see that they are just like I am, they need a way to understand the empirical evidence they see, and their philosophy is Evolution. In today's culture, my views are looked at as my Christian Bias at work, but everyone has a bias of some sort it's just recognizing it for what it is.

Having a solid base of philosophy to understand real empirical evidence is something I need and have seen others need as well. I do not condemn people for their philosophy, because what I have learned is we all need a philosophical understanding to evidences presented to us of things as diverse as Scientific Data, religious ethical studies, or even how to eat healthy. If we do not have a philosophy then we are not compelled to do anything about what is seen by empirical evidence. True Science is an unnecessary endeavour without a philosophy to understand and use the data.

Do you think a Creationist would be excited to find a new layer of never before seen fossils? They wouldn't, because it would mean that a non-evolution theory may be proven wrong. The Evolutionist however, if he found a layer of fossils which could explain the transitional beings which evolution needs to have, would be so excited he/she would work until all the data was uncovered and published.

This type of reasoning is why I see Philosophy being as important to us as the data itself. Without philosophy our motivations become non-existent.

Judaic reasoning and logic is the best perspective, in my opinion, to combat the coming tide of secularism, and the relatively quick removal of Christian truth from the halls of Academia, within Christian or Secular schools, and into the dustbin of history.

Christianity is innately tied to Greek thinking. Democratic and Capitalistic ideology has come from the Romans, and this philosophy has been around for over 2500 years.

Democracy started in the Greek Isles and was transformed into a monolithic philosophy by the intellectuals of the Roman Empire. When the Empire had already been split and was becoming even weaker, a visionary leader decided to use a Messianic Cult to push his Democratic ideals.

Emperor Constantine saw that the majority of the Empire believed in too many different philosophies which made too many dangerous factions to manage. He wanted to consolidate the people into one religion in order to gain more control. Make no mistake, Constantine was an Emperor first and follower of Religion second or third in perspective of his life. Power came first in his heart and mind.

The Church became, because of his idea of consolidation, something of a good thing to be a part of. The leaders of the Church, who were few, had power they never had before.

They needed to make their religion palatable to a Roman audience because of this vote of confidence from Constantine. Instead of following the Apostles doctrines of peace and love of others, with no kingdom building, the leaders of the Church in 325 had to take a different approach.

Constantine chose a path of kingdom building for the leaders, and made them force their perspective on the known world, making the church leaders elitists, even if they didn't want to be elitists. This ideology of elitism has taken hold and is as deep as anything else in the Christian Church.

In the past 100 years however, this Greek ideology of elitism has been seeing a decline within every sector it is dominant. From Italy to Spain, to North America and Asia, Greek thinking in a Christian context is becoming something people are embarrassed to admit to.

A new age of Philosophical freedom has come and we as a church need to realize were we stand. The Greek elitist ideology we have stood in for 1500 years is becoming passé and changing back to what it was when Plato and Socrates wrote about it, which means that the pantheon of god's (now referred to more as lifestyle choices) mindset is coming back.

The Church has also gone through many changes since the third Century when this elitist philosophy became the dominant way to think about the church. We have had no central government in the church to speak of, for over 1000 years. There have been three main governments of the church (Roman Catholic, Eastern Orthodox, and independent bodies). We have however, from around the 2$^{nd}$ Century until now believed basically the same things because of the inherent Greek logic within Christian Doctrine.

We all feel the husband is the head of the home (meaning the husband makes all decisions) thus introducing this elitist view in the very basic part of Society. We all look to a Pastor or Priest as the expert for Biblical truth. We all believe in a creedal perspective of belief whether formal or informal. We all believe in some sort of hierarchical system of government. These all come from Greek Religion, not from Judaic thought. The Church was married to this philosophical approach around 1500 years ago.

The world in the preceding 1000 years, at least in a Western Context, used the Churches dogma as the preeminent philosophy of doing Society. The morals, laws, family structure, and overall fabric of society went through a prism of biblical understanding to make up its laws and code of ethics, this is referred to as Judeo-Christian ethics, and it is now ending.

In almost every European Nation there was a State Religion, and within this was taught the morality for the State. When the United States was formed it was to break away from this control of Religion by the State. They formed a Union where every Biblically based religion had equal rights, but they still derived their moral structure from the different Churches of the States or Cities. Canada was also based on Religious freedoms as given by the Royals of England.

Now however, the Moral compass for doing Society is changing. The changes are not small changes either. Greek philosophy of elitism that was used to give Society its form is now being reduced to one which has no power in regard to morality and laws. The Greek elitist philosophy the 4<sup>th</sup> Century Believers were so enamored with has now become the ball and chain which will sink the churches most important doctrines and beliefs because Greek thinking has a bedrock in a pantheon of god's, which now means a pantheon of belief's.

This means that Greek philosophy allows for different beliefs as long as it keeps the elitist structure. Belief in Messiah is not important as long as elitism is controlling the people. The Church has become divided because of this but looks lost with respect to leadership because the World paints us as backwards because we do accept real science.

The first and foremost truth is that believers take Biblical truths as a way of life. When elitists tell us that our bedrocks of belief is at odds with empirical evidence, churches who have fully embraced Greek thinking can adapt to the new rules (look at the Anglicans and Methodists as pictures of what I mean), but churches which believe half in Judaic thought and half in Greek are finding it difficult to adapt to the cultural norms (look at Catholic, Baptist,

Mennonite, Pentecostal, Brethren, Evangelical, and Independent Bible based churches to see what I mean).

There is an old adage in the Scriptures given by Paul where he said,

*"When I was a child, I talked like a child; I thought like a child, I reasoned like a child. When I became a man, I put the ways of childhood behind me"*

The Bible has concrete empirical philosophical underpinnings that cannot be changed because of someone's belief in evolution or a revised understanding of DNA. The Bible is very clear on certain things when understood in its original context, to remove it from its original context is dangerous, because it changes the outcome of what it brings mankind.

The Greek mentality is dangerous to a Biblical Worldview because it starts by studying the core sciences, then enters into a philosophy which fits the perspective of what that core science perspective gives you, then you finish with a mystery belief which is ultimately personal. This belief does not necessarily have to be based on anything but your own perspective of what you deem as true. This is very dangerous to our children because it leaves them with no legacy except questions of what is true. We are raising children who mirror Pontius Pilate, who asked Jesus the question of "What is truth?", more than the Apostle Peter who proclaimed truth fearlessly.

The Judaic way of thinking for me, is much more logical and conducive to building a belief system upon because it requires at its core a belief in an unseen Creator as spoken of in the Bible. In the next few chapters I will try to explain why I feel the Church fell into Greek philosophy rather than stay with its roots which were Judaic. The Church says Paul was the reason but I will present another reason.

# Chapter 3

## Does the Church have a Problem?

You may be asking me, if there are so many problems in how the Church thinks then why are the churches growing in numbers? In the past 100 years of the Church (in this chapter my reference to Church means not just people who believe but the actual organizations of believers) in North America, we have seen unprecedented growth. There are now over 55,000 registered Christian Denominations within Canada and the United States. This is a staggering number.

I am not speaking about churches as one congregation here, but denominations. Usually a denomination is defined as a group of people who believe a certain way about the Bible. Many are very similar, and non-Christians would be hard pressed to see any difference between them but within Believing circles this number of denominations mean that the message has gotten out. Most denominations have several churches, some do not of course, but if we say an average sized church is around 150 people, and multiply that number by 10 churches per separate Denomination as an average, this is around 85-100 million people. Out of the 400 million people that are in Canada and the United States, these are the people in the pews every Sunday.

This means approximately 1 in 4 people attend church in North America, or around 25% of the people in North America is attending a church service on Sunday, probably more, because these numbers are not completely scientific. Wikipedia says that 46% of people surveyed in a Gallup poll said they attend church sometime in the year, but when you break it down to regular attendees then it is 26%. Either way this is a big number of people attending Church. Why do I believe the church is not thinking right when they are doing well numbers wise?

My thoughts are simple; let's see how alike to the World the Church is, by church this time I mean all the denominations together, the people who have become a member of a church, not just the people who believe in their hearts.

The Apostle Paul said in Romans 12:2 that we should not conform ourselves to the patterns of the World. How can we judge whether or not we are close to the World, again I think the simple approach is the easiest.

1. What is the churches divorce rates, are we a committed people to the basic building block of society according to Scripture? The Barna Group found out that amongst all Christian churches whether Protestant or Catholic the percentages of divorces are around 32-35% for first marriages there are no stats for second or third. North American average for divorces is 41% for first marriages, and amazingly enough 56% of people divorce in their second marriages and 73% for third marriages, not much of a difference.

2. How many people in church know that Jesus taught about whole-hearted devotion (John 14)? Difficult to gauge, most people in church, unless they are in leadership seem to side with their particular brand of religion, as with anything it is difficult to know and only Jesus ultimately can decide, but we know in our hearts if we are following

with our whole heart, or just mouthing the words, it is something only we can answer individually. We need however to see the percentages of people who share their faith, ones who help the homeless, or the people of the Church who actually live during the week what they say they believe on Sunday. There is a business principle that says 20% of the people do 80% of the work and 80% of the people do 20% of the work. Within the Church this is played out every Sunday.

3. How many Believers in church understand what a Disciple is? Difficult to gauge, but let's say 30% are Disciples in church, and then we have much smaller number of people who believe.

4. And finally, how many people in Church are not self-centered but honestly think of others before themselves? Difficult to gauge but when I see all these bless me clubs which are called churches I surmise the number of people who consider others over themselves is low. I could be wrong as no one knows what's in the heart.

---

With the numbers of attendees so high, these principles should be seen on a much larger scale than we are seeing now within the World. When I see the homeless shelters around the world I see that they are still short on workers, when I see the set-up crews in churches there are still only certain people who help. When I see churches use their money to take care of their own only rather than the needy in their Community I see that the principles of others first is rarely done in churches, this to me speaks of a gap in whole hearted devotion.

The Lord has a common standard for those who follow Him, we need to rally around it, no matter what we call ourselves, or what culture we are from. I believe that the standard of interpretation adopted 1500 years ago is not valid because it allows for the Cultural truths to become preeminent within the church.

When I was in Bible College the only consistent truth I saw was that most of the people followed a Greek way of thinking. Plato said that writing was not a good medium of communication, he thought speaking was much better and said that he had secret knowledge which no one could know because it was his secret knowledge.

I find that we as Christians have adopted this same type of mystery belief after we learn the understandings of the Bible. What happens is we become secretive and closed off because after you have sit in church for about five years you have learned most of what it has to offer. Consequently, we all as believers become distant from the Lord, or lose our first love. This does not have to happen.

Right now the Lord is opening our hearts as a Church to become Berean's, the people Paul commended in Acts 17:10-15, and look into how we have been studying. I am not talking about the intelligentsia of our day, or the professionals. I am talking about each and every person who has been changed by a personal encounter with the Lord Jesus Christ.

No one is perfect in this, and least of all me, but todays church cares more about what the Lord can do for them then what He wants to do through them. For God to work through us means he wants to use our lives to bless others. We are not the center of the universe He is.

Why do we have almost the same divorce numbers as the World? Why do so many people go from one Church to another when they get mad or bored? Why do we insist that we can be believers but not engage in discipleship or full repentance, and stubbornly cling to our old ways of life? Why are we as a people always gossiping and bickering with one another and never coming to solutions?

I personally believe this is because we have forsaken Torah Principles; we have taken out the basic ethical teachings of the Scriptures and replaced them with pop cultural psychological answers. This comes from a Greek view of life.

Ten years ago there was a major upheaval in views on historical Israel, and Judaism in particular. Many Messianic groups were formed in this time, and there were many churches and church people who realized Judaism was not what they had always thought it was. I even read many discussions in Theology papers of how we failed to see that Israel is different than the Church.

There are over 12 major Prophecies (10 were fulfilled in just one day in 1948 when Israel became a Sovereign Nation) that can only be about the twelve tribes of Israel, unless you change who

Israel is. For the people who say Israel has been replaced by a group of Gentiles, they usually do not take the Bible in context or end up reducing the Old Testament covenants and promises Israel received into a box of dispensational idiocy.

Every denomination who declares that the Jew (a descendant of Judah) or other family member from the other 12 sons of Jacob need to believe in Jesus to get to heaven is completely misunderstanding what the bible teaches about belief in Israel's Messiah.

Let me explain it this way, is Jesus Israel's Messiah? Yes, do the Jews believe in Israel's Messiah, Yes they do, it is their 12th Principle of faith. Do they follow Jesus as we do, no, but why cannot we accept them for who they are and stop comparing ourselves to them and vice versa? We are all saved by believing in the Messiah of Israel, not following Him.

Why do the Jews not believe in Jesus as we do? First they do not see Him as we do yet. They see a soon coming Messiah who will set up a Messianic Kingdom, is this Jesus, yes it is. There are blinders on most of the Jews eyes with respect to their Messiah's first time here on Earth. These will come off if we as Gentiles do our job as Paul entreats us in Romans 11:11, we need to provoke them to jealousy.

We do not need to take away their Talmud, or drown them in barrels of water (this is what our great reformer Martin Luther loved to do), or tell them they are second class citizens, or call ourselves Israel because somehow they lost the title when Jesus came. We shouldn't say that the Jews are our biggest enemies and forbid their Rabbis to teach, or shove them away into a filthy part of the City where they are restricted to buy anything but garbage.

We should show them how their Messiah has brought us into the same intimate relationship with God as they have. We should show them that we know the Torah, and love the Torah just as much as them, and we never were at the foot of Mt Sinai to say, "I will do and I will obey". And yet we still follow.

It is very ignorant in my mind, for men and women, who believe they are well read, and highly educated to discount 5,000 years of historical teachings from people who were given the Word of God, but this is what about 85% of the Christian Church has done. Regardless of your view on Scripture, there are too many incontrovertible truths declaring Israel and the 12 tribes of people who sprung from Jacobs's loins to be God's chosen people, not a group of gentiles who somehow took the Hebrew Scriptures and reinterpreted them for themselves through a Greek translation.

In essence, what the Church has done would be like if another Country, one like China or India, who have a greater population, took the Constitution of the United States and said it was actually written for them because they were truly a free society and can interpret its laws properly, whereas the USA is definitely not abiding by its premises so therefore its laws has nothing to do with them anymore, nor the promise of societal order it carries.

Americans would probably do the same thing Israel does to the church, laugh at them for their ignorance, then try to explain to them what the Constitution really stands for, who wrote it, what it was really for, and how it fits life today. As the Church, we need to realize that the Jews are the chosen people not us, we are grafted in.

We as the grafted in shoot, have done nothing to cause the Jewish person to be jealous of our relationship with the Lord. We are proud, arrogant, and believe we are the only ones God loves. We couch these attitudes in phrases like "I just believe in Jesus and they do not, I didn't make the rules I only follow them".

Or we say "Acts says there is only ONE Name under Heaven by which we are saved, it's not Torah." These are absurd when you realize who Israel is, and what God has said about them. Israel is already in a relationship with God, and God says because of Him they will be brought back, not because of their works (Psalm 89:30-37, Amos 9:14-15).

Here are some verses to chew on for the people who say Israel has been replaced by Gentiles. These verses are extremely hard to refute about Israel's (the physical descendants of the twelve Sons of Jacob) continued favor of God.

*Isaiah 40:1-2, "Comfort, comfort my people, says your God. Speak tenderly to Jerusalem, and proclaim to her that her hard service has been completed, that her sin has been paid for, that she has received from the Lord's hand double for all her sins."*

*Isaiah 62:6-7, "I have posted watchmen on your walls, O Jerusalem; they will never be silent day or night. You who call on the Lord, give yourselves no rest, and give him no rest till he establishes Jerusalem and makes her the praise of the earth."*

*Jeremiah 31:31-32 "The time is coming," declares the Lord, "when I will make a new covenant with the house of Israel and with the house of Judah. It will not be like the covenant I made with their forefathers when I took them by the hand to lead them out of Egypt, because they broke my covenant, though I was a husband to them," declares the Lord.*

*Ezekiel 36:24, "'For I will take you out of the nations; I will gather you from all the countries and bring you back into your own land'"*

As Paul says 'may it never be that Israel has fallen as to never recover.' We should reach out to our brothers and learn from them so that they can see God is with us as well. Right now the normal Orthodox Jewish man would tell us that we worship 3 Gods, which is something he couldn't do. We look and sound very much like the Romans who kicked his ancestors out of Israel in the first place. We do not follow the Bible in the way Moses handed it down so why would he be jealous of us.

The Orthodox Jew, the one Paul was entreating us to minister to is far removed from our radar; we consider them somehow less than us. I say woe unto any man who looks down on the Jew, because they were the ones who God entrusted His Words, not us. I used to get into heated arguments with fellow Believers over my stance on Israel.

Whenever I would bring up Israel and how the Jews were Gods chosen people, someone would tell me that they were left in a historical trashbin somewhere, and had no place in Gods plans, then these people would vehemently argue with me as we went through the scriptures to which proves Israel is still Gods Chosen People. These same people would then say with excitement in their voice that if the Jews get saved it's another story of course, but until the prayer of salvation is made from their lips they are outside of God. I found this to be ludicrous, and even more so now, after studying what the Jew actually believes about salvation and the Messiah of Israel.

I know these statements are quite controversial, but look deeply into who Israel is and come to your own conclusion. I beg you, do not take only your denominations perspective, make sure when you stand before the Lord on judgment day you can stand there with them in the belief that only Christians will be found to be worthy to be in heaven because of a prayer of salvation, or because of following a Christian Creed.

I am not saying here that salvation does not come through the Messiah who we know is Jesus, what I am saying is that belief in the Messiah may be different for the Jew than the Gentile. It is this belief in the Messiah which brings salvation not some magical incantation which usher us into His Kingdom.

I am trying to be clear on the fact that Israel is God's chosen Nation. God's chosen people are not some loosely gathered together gentiles from many nations who built a kingdom in Jesus' name. We as Believers in the Messiah are like the Samaritans who set up their own Temple, you can build it and say it's real but it doesn't make it true. Israel has been around for over 5,000 years and looks like it will be here another 5,000 if need be. God has them in His hand and no one will pluck him out (Isa. 43-45).

When we realize collectively that God called Israel into being, just like he called us into a relationship with His Son, we will stop being so arrogant and proud and live the life the Lord wants us to. We are trying to build an Earthly Kingdom rather than a Spiritual Kingdom. The Lord Jesus was not setting up an Earthly Kingdom. Remember, He chose us, not the other way around. God also chose Israel to carry His Words and be redeemed because of the promises He had given to them.

In the next Chapter, I want to lay out my argument for why Peter could not have used a Greek way to come to his understanding of how to live. From there I will try to explain why Jesus was more of a Pharisee than a Theologian or Pastor of today.

# Chapter 4

## Is Peter the Head of the Church?

Matthew 16:13-20 *"When Jesus came to the region of Caesarea Philippi, he asked his disciples, "Who do people say the Son of Man is?"[14]They replied, "Some say John the Baptist others say Elijah; and still others, Jeremiah or one of the prophets."[15]"But what about you?" he asked. "Who do you say I am?"[16]Simon Peter answered, "You are the Messiah, the Son of the living God."[17]Jesus replied, "Blessed are you, Simon son of Jonah, **for this was not revealed to you by flesh and blood, but by my Father in heaven.[18]And I tell you that you are Peter, and on this rock I will build my church, and the gates of Hades will not overcome it.[19]**I will give you the keys of the kingdom of heaven; whatever you bind on earth will be bound in heaven, and whatever you loose on earth will be loosed in heaven."[20]Then he ordered his disciples not to tell anyone that he was the Messiah*

Let us first look at Peter; he was essentially an uneducated fisherman who was one of the first men to be called a Disciple of Jesus. He is known as the one who was impetuous, emotional, and someone who wanted to be the leader. Jesus seemed to take a special liking to him and called him into a leadership circle of 3, which consisted of Peter, James, and John. This is the traditional perspective of what the scriptures say.

Before I start I have to clarify something about the Catholic version of what it means when Jesus proclaimed "on this Rock" (Matt 16:18). The Catholics insist it meant Peter himself, rather than the statement Peter had uttered. What I mean by this is instead of interpreting the phrase in verse 18 as meaning the belief in Jesus as Messiah; the Catholic Church says it means Peter and his leadership.

They believe the rock on which the Church will be built upon is Peter, and then put him as the head of the Church. They vociferously insist that the first believers believed this as well. This idea subtly changes the perspective from being a heart belief and personal, into more of believing in an ideology and group of men who tell you what to do. It puts more emphasis on the person you follow, rather than what you follow, this is very important for our children's generation to realize.

If Jesus meant that Peter was the rock, and He wanted us to follow a person, it means that Jesus wanted people to rally around a

Kinglike being. We need to ask, did Jesus want to set up a kingdom, or was he showing the Nation of Israel and the people that would follow afterward what it would take to be His follower?

It does sound like Jesus is referring to Peter in verse 18, but it is not because of who Peter is, but what he said he believed. This is very important to realize. Peter's belief has to be the main thing here not him as a person, or Jesus' and the Apostles other teachings about belief being the key become meaningless.

The subtle shift the Catholic Church introduces here in the text also creates an elitist view of the leaders of the church. This thinking that there needs to be a head of the Church seems to be contrary to the purpose of this passage. To believe this was about how Jesus was setting up His church seems to miss the point entirely of what Jesus was trying to get across.

Jesus, in my mind was trying to see if the Disciples truly believed, or was just following because of the miracles. In the verses preceding the confession Peter gave, Jesus was trying to make the Disciples see that it is not Physical which is important, but instead it is belief (Matthew 16:1-12).

Within the Roman mentality of that day, order was above all else. They believed honor must be given to teachers, and this honor meant the teachers were above students. Knowledge and connections equaled power within a Greek worldview, especially in Rome at this time.

Jesus explained in Matthew to the other Disciples why they should not be jealous of James and John's Mother asking Him to give her Sons special advancement and placement in His Kingdom. Here is what Jesus said about His Kingdoms overall ideology on Leadership.

Matthew 20: 24-28, *²⁴When the ten heard about this, they were indignant with the two brothers.²⁵Jesus called them together and said, "You know that the rulers of the **Gentiles lord it over them**, and their high officials exercise authority over them.²⁶**Not so with you.** Instead, whoever wants to become great among you must be your servant,²⁷and **whoever wants to be first must be your slave**—²⁸just as the Son of Man did not come to be served, but to serve, and to give his life as a ransom for many."*

Peter also weighed in on this,

1 Peter 5:1-6, *"To the elders among you, I appeal as a* ***fellow elder*** *and a witness of Christ's sufferings who also will share in the glory to be revealed:* [2]***Be shepherds of God's flock*** *that is under your care, watching over them—* ***not because you must, but because you are willing***, *as God wants you to be; not pursuing dishonest gain, but eager to serve;* [3]***not lording it over those entrusted to you, but being examples to the flock.*** [4]*And when the Chief Shepherd appears, you will receive the crown of glory that will never fade away.* [5]*In the same way, you who are younger, submit yourselves to your elders. All of you,* ***clothe yourselves with humility toward one another, because, "God opposes the proud but shows favor to the humble"*** [6]***Humble yourselves, therefore, under God's mighty hand, that he may lift you up in due time."***

Jesus and the Apostle Peter did not consider themselves as leaders in the conventual way, they considered themselves as servants. You have to put yourself in the shoes of these men.

They could have set up a large kingdom with the normal hierarchy of the day, but instead chose to follow Torah Principles which would not allow these things. In the

Torah Moses was not the General, but instead was the Servant of the people.

The Jews of the 1<sup>st</sup> Century seemed to also have the mentality that learned leaders were above the students or 'the regular people', but this was wrong, and Jesus on numerous occasions explained why. He also rebuked the people strongly who were engaged in these practices.

If we look at why the people who followed God within Israel were always persecuted it was because they never asserted their authority over others, they instead served others which made them easy targets to be persecuted. Jesus taught that this was the proper path of leadership, become the servant, not the lord.

I do not believe that Jesus was setting up a kingdom; it was completely contrary to His goals during his Ministry here on Earth. Here are His goals as stated within Matthew 23:37-39

*<sup>37</sup> "Jerusalem, Jerusalem, you who kill the prophets and stone those sent to you, how often **I have longed to gather your children together, as a hen gathers her chicks under her wings, and you were not willing**.<sup>38</sup>Look, your house is left to you desolate.<sup>39</sup>For I tell you, you will not see me again until you say, 'Blessed is he who comes in the name of the Lord.'*

When people rally around one person and put one life ahead of others it causes us as to have an elitist attitude which is contrary to the Gospel. Jesus wanted his Disciple's to do first, then teach, not teach and not do. This understanding of power is important in our discussion because it has been this type of elitist view that was built into the Church which I believe is contrary to its message.

If you are lost in what the Catholics believe about Peter the Apostle, I suggest you ask a Priest to explain to you how Popes, Priests, Nuns, and the like have come into being, then study the critics version, and finally look at the history of how they came into being, it is a very eye opening study. Most of the hierarchical understandings introduced to us came from understanding this Scripture verse, through this Greek way of interpretation.

There is an elitist view in Judaism today of the Rabbis and Rebbe's, but it is closer to the honor the Apostles taught needed to be given to the leaders, than the Churches Hierarchical system which is about power more than honor.

The Chasidic movement has gone very far in elevating 2 sections of the Rabbinical Hierarchy. The Rebbe (or main leader of a Community) and the Tzaddik (or Righteous One) are seen as Mystical Torah experts who are able to almost be the voice of God for people. Some people within Judaism do not like this elevating of the Rabbi's but realize it is a natural thing to do and try to teach about respect rather than blind allegiance.

Here are some quotes from the Talmud on how deep the Sages wanted to teach reverence for teachers, but they also had a realistic view of the power they wielded.

*The Sages of the Gemara spoke most emphatically about teaching about the importance of Jewish schoolchildren. One passage alone contains three statements about it:*

*Rabbi Yehudah said in the name of Rav: "What is meant by the verse 'Do not touch My anointed ones' (Divrei HaYamimI16:22)? It refers to tinokos shel beis rabban [tashbar]."*

*Rabbi Hamnuna said: "Yerushalayim was destroyed only because they suspended the schoolchildren." [This does not mean that children were expelled from school for bad behavior; it means they stopped teaching them.]*

*And even such pronouncements are not to be compared to*
*that of Reish Lakish in the name of Rabbi Yehudah HaNassi: "The*
*world is sustained only because of the breath of the schoolchildren*
*[expelled when they learn Torah]."(Shabbos 119b)*

This quote goes to the idea which is common in Judaism that the Rabbi is the one person who can bring about what is called Olam Ha Ba or The World to Come. Here is a good quote from the Talmud on what is understood of Olam Ha Ba.

*"This world is like a lobby before the Olam Ha-Ba.*
*Prepare yourself in the lobby so that you may enter the banquet*
*hall."*

Similarly, the Talmud says,

*"This world is like the eve of Shabbat, and the Olam Ha-*
*Ba is like Shabbat. He who prepares on the eve of Shabbat will*
*have food to eat on Shabbat." We prepare ourselves for the Olam*
*Ha-Ba through Torah study and good deeds.*

I think that if we honestly look at how the Jewish people view teachers we can see that within Judaism the teacher was respected but only in regards to how the students grew in their Torah learning. If the Torah Teacher did not teach them how to live a Torah Lifestyle, he wasn't honored, thus had no voice in the Community. This means the Rabbi had to not only speak the words properly, but also live the words he was speaking. There are of course exceptions to this rule but the ideology is much closer to what Jesus was teaching about what it means to be a leader.

If we look at Jesus' teachings on this discussion, he made it very clear that the Teacher should wash the feet of the student; teaching is ultimately a service to a person. The teacher should never be seen as something like a lord. This lording it over the student is where the teacher student relationship went off the rails for the Church and Judaism.

Jesus taught in Mark 10:42-44, *"42 Jesus called them together and said, "You know that those who are regarded as rulers of the Gentiles lord it over them, and their high officials exercise authority over them. 43 Not so with you. Instead, whoever wants to become great among you must be your servant, 44 and whoever wants to be first must be slave of all.45 For even the Son of Man did not come to be served, but to serve, and to give his life as a ransom for many."* how wrong the Gentiles were when they set up this type of structure. I believe He was specifically referring to the way the Romans viewed a teacher student relationship, one in which the teacher lorded their authority over their students, much like the Church has become now.

It is ironic that Socrates and Plato did not teach that the teacher should lord it over the student, but believed that the Teacher should be a friend and mentor to the student so the student learns in every part of his life.

The Sophists in Rome were the ones who introduced the concept of tuition and made general curriculums for teaching. The Sophist's were the first people who started education for the masses because of this type of education.

Sophists didn't care for their student's needs and only taught the subjects they were paid to teach, which meant they made their curriculum in a general way, not specific to the student's needs as Socrates and Plato thought was best. This model is what has made learning into what it is today, not the intimate one it should be, but a general curriculum.

This has worked to educate the masses, but it somehow misses something. Without this however most would still be uneducated, I am not saying this is a bad system, I am just showing that the Greek thinking infiltrated the Church and took over its systems.

Jesus taught that care and friendship comes first in the student-teacher relationship. Jesus taught the model of Apprenticeship over curriculum. It means that the teacher was a servant to the student, which in the 1$^{st}$ Century meant a much different concept than today. The Apostles did teach that leaders were worthy of pay and respect, but this did not mean they were lords over the others, it meant that because the teacher gave their whole time to teach they needed a way to feed themselves and families.

Jesus also taught his disciples leadership positions were not his to give, but only God could appoint these jobs. Even He as a Messiah and part of the Godhead could not lord his authority over anyone, but had to serve the truth He was bringing, which meant if John and James were not worthy to be the leaders than they wouldn't be, it was not up to Him to appoint them.

When I read the notion of John and James Mom trying to get Jesus to appoint them, I did not see her as a power hungry person, but someone who wanted her sons to always be near their Lord and

Messiah. Jesus however used the question to turn the whole concept of preparation for leadership on its head by saying it was up to the Father and who would become leaders. Basically, He said no matter how much education, power, or influence a person had it came down to the Fathers blessing not a man's.

What I desire to establish here in this chapter is the thought that there are 2 ways of interpreting the truth of the Scriptures, there is a Judaic way and a Platonic or Greek way. We as one of the final generations of believers have the duty to use this time of explosive knowledge and relative freedom of thought to set aside our prejudices and follow truth no matter where it is. Let's get back to Peter.

Peter was one of the main leaders of the Disciples when Jesus was here on Earth, but it appears he was relegated to being just one of many leaders once the Apostles were established. The main leader in Jerusalem was Jesus' own Brother James, who was killed by Herod's High Priest before the diaspora began.

Several historians, the first being Hegesippus a Jewish Believer and 2nd Century Historian, wrote that James, Jesus' brother, was the leader of the Church and died by being thrown from the pinnacle of the Temple for giving testimony of Jesus as the Christ.

The 4th Century Historian Eusebius supports the view that the James was Jesus' brother by quoting from the 1st Century Clements's account. Paul also says that Jesus first appeared to Cephas or Peter (Luke 24:34), then the 11 (Luke 24:31), then to 500 of His followers (Luke 24:36-51, I Cor 15:3-7), then to James (I Cor 15:7), all of the Apostles again (1 Cor 15:7), and finally to Paul himself as one abnormally born (I Cor. 15:8). Putting James by himself probably means he was the Leader of the Congregation.

Peter, as far as we know through the Scriptures and other ancient writings, was never the sole leader of the Church in Jerusalem, according to most church historians and manuscripts we have, Peter was always a respected voice, and one who the believers and leaders went to for guidance and confirmation of the Lords words, but his duty was as an Apostle. When we look at what it meant to be an Apostle, it was simply being an Emissary of the Gospel.

To be an Emissary did not carry some great spiritual weight to it, it only meant that they had to go to places which were difficult to live, and be a witness that Jesus had come in the flesh. Here is some testimony by Paul of what being an Apostle meant in reality,

1 Corinthians 4:1-2, & 9-13, "*1This, then, is how you ought to regard us: as **servants of Christ** and as **those entrusted with the mysteries God has revealed.**2Now it is required that those who have been given a trust must prove faithful.*

*9For it seems to me that **God has put us apostles on display at the end of the procession**, like those condemned to die in the arena. **We have been made a spectacle to the whole universe**, to angels as well as to human beings.10**We are fools for Christ**, but you are so wise in Christ! **We are weak**, but you are strong! You are honored, we are dishonored!11To this very hour we **go hungry and thirsty, we are in rags, we are brutally treated, and we are homeless.**12**We work hard with our own hands. When we are cursed, we bless; when we are persecuted, we endure it;**13 **when we are slandered, we answer kindly. We have become the scum of the earth, the garbage of the world**—right up to this moment.14I am writing this not to shame you but to warn you as my dear children.15Even if you had ten thousand guardians in*

*Christ, you do not have many fathers, for in Christ Jesus **I became your***

***father through the gospel.***"

Apostles were not the celebrated super-humans that the Church thinks they were. They were men endued with the Holy Spirit who had a rough life spreading the Gospel throughout a pagan culture. They had victories, but also many defeats. What made them Apostles was not who they were, but what they believed. They did not want to change the status quo, but instead they wanted to share the love of Christ, that is all.

The Elitism which cropped up later was not because of their words, they would have been astounded being called a Prince or being brought into fine dining experiences because of the titles they held. They wanted to only show the World who Jesus was and that He walked on this planet.

The Catholic Church writings have Peter as the first Pope of Rome; they even have him establishing the Church in Rome. My first question arises from the fact that he wrote his Epistles from Babylon (1 Peter 5:13). Being in Babylon, which was a province of what is present day Iraq would make much more sense because that is where the Jews went to escape the Romans, and developed what would be known as the Babylonian Talmud there. Paul in his writings never once mentions Peter is with him. I would think that if Paul and Peter were in Rome at the same time he would mention this.

Whenever Paul mentioned Peter, he was in Jerusalem. I do not think Peter would have wanted to go to Rome, but this is only my opinion. Rome was an anathema to the Jews, and Peter was one leader of a new sect of Judaism, his own calling according to Paul in Galatians 2:8-10 was to the Jews, as was John, and James Jesus' Brother.

It's difficult to see how Peter became the super Pope he has been made out to be, but I guess if you tell a lie long enough most people will believe it is true. Why is this important to discuss?

It is important because the Church in Rome, which became Roman Catholics, needed to have a King like man in order to set up their own Kingdom. When the church became the State Religion with Emperor Constantine it had none of these ideas, or even wanted them.

Without changing the truth of "on this rock" statement, there could be no kingdom. With the change in meaning, it opened up the idea for a Kingdom, as well as a change over from Judaic thought to Greek esoteric philosophy and ethics.

Jesus wanted the Apostles first of all to be servants. Jesus taught them that servanthood was the preeminent hallmark of a Godly man, not someone who sat at the head of the table. In fairness to the ones who would say the Apostles did sit at the head of the tables in respect to deciding the fate of the Believers. I would remind them in Acts 15 James, Jesus' brother, decided what would be written. It was not the Apostle Peter, or the Apostle Andrew, or the Apostle James son of Zebedee or the Apostle John his brother, it was James.

Here in Acts 6:1-4, *"In those days when the number of disciples was increasing, the Hellenistic Jews among them complained against the Hebraic Jews because their widows were being overlooked in the daily distribution of food. [2] So the Twelve gathered all the disciples together and said, "It would not be right for us to neglect the ministry of the word of God in order to wait on tables. [3] Brothers and sisters, choose seven men from among you who are known to be full of the Spirit and wisdom. We will turn this responsibility over to them [4] and will give our attention to prayer and the ministry of the word. "*, we see that the Apostles were the ones who distributed the food as well teach the Word of God, which meant the Torah. It's interesting that the Church never explains the Apostles were the servants of all. All we hear about is how they taught the Word of God with power, saw people healed, and were super human in respect to suffering. Until the Apostles realized they were not serving the people properly with respect to food disbursements, they didn't realize they needed help in the serving the new believers.

The reality is that the Apostles were the hardest working people in the Church, not just men who studied, taught, and prayed for people, but men who cooked, cleaned, and gave money when it was needed. They were the examples of the teachings, not because of some hope to be someone, but because of a character refined by fire and wholehearted devotion to their Messiah, Brother, and Friend.

As a follow up to who Peter was, we see in Scripture that Peter was spoken of as an Apostle to the Jews (Gal. 2:8), Paul as an Apostle to the Gentiles (Acts 9:15), and it seems that Thomas was an Apostle to the Indian Subcontinent, and other Apostles were spoken of in various archaeological finds being sent to other areas for Ministry. This picture of where the Apostles fit in with respect to their areas of calling to today's callings on men as well.

I know people like a Fijian who was called to go from a small fishing Village in Fiji that had no electricity, to preaching the Gospel in Nepal. I also know of a Samoan who was called to Bangladesh to preach the Gospel, and has spent his whole life there. There is no pride in these people of thinking they are some superhuman leaders of Gods Church in Nepal and Bangladesh, they just serve by doing whatever is necessary to get the gospel out to people who have never heard. Neither of these men had the money nor the financial backing needed to see the fruit they have had in their Ministry, but what they did have was a calling and refined character to meet the requirements the Lord asked of them in these fields. Now is no different from then, we are all serving the same Lord, and He does the same things in our lives He did in the first generations of people's lives. It's not because of who we are, but who He is.

I think with the meagre evidence historically and Scripturally, (except the volumes of teachings the Catholic Church has made to try and prove otherwise), each Apostle had a field they were sent to and were far from being Chief Shepard's, Princes, Bishops, or even Pastors, but instead Apostles plain and simple.

I believe, contrary to today's elitist views of Church leaders, this meant they were the chief servants, just normal people who knew Jesus and were consumed by preaching His Gospel, in whatever manner that entailed.

These men started groups of believers, sometimes only the slaves would hear so they would serve the slaves (unheard of until they did it I might add), and then after a solid core of believers were started they left leaders who carried the leadership burden.

If there were problems or there needed confirmation of Jesus' Words then the Apostles were consulted, but the day to day Ministry was handled by the leaders which were left in the towns and villages that had the Communities. The leaders in the Communities had more say in the life of the believer than the Apostles, who were busy preaching and starting new communities.

We also need to remember that the church was not monolithic, which simply means that it had many different aspects to it and was not one giant organism. It took 3-4 centuries before there were set doctrines agreed upon by all the Churches. The different Church Councils came about because when Constantine gave the Church the leadership role of the Empire's official Religion, Christianity had to be more organized.

Until the 3rd Century and the council of Nicaea in AD 325, the different churches did not look to one man or one group of men for a rubber stamp on what they believed. Even after this council there was still no single man in charge of the structure of the Church. The Church was a very fluid organism and usually responded to the needs of the people it served, very rarely going out of its own area of influence.

There are many reasons for this, but I believe one reason for the fluid aspect of the Church was the men and women who knew Jesus as their Messiah were content in their own churches and were active Disciples, they didn't want a Kingdom as is known on Earth, but were waiting for the Kingdom Jesus was bringing.

Back to Peter, everyone who reads the Gospels, or Peters Letters can see that he was insignificant with respect to the intelligentsia of his day, which were comprised of the Pharisees, Sadducees, Priests, and the other more fringe groups like the Herodians, Essenes, and Dead Sea Scroll groups who are not named in Scripture that we have.

In this time frame, Israel had some of their most renowned leaders and scholars, true sages of Judaism, men like Gamaliel, Hillel, Shammai, Yochanan ben Zakai, and Rabbi Akiba. These were men who energized, as well as solidified Judaism teachings from then until now. Peter being a Fisherman with only 3 years under a Master would never have been able to stand shoulder to shoulder with these giants, but he was called to do just this.

Peter was someone who was passionate but not educated enough to be the top leader of a new Messianic group. Without the Catholic Churches insistence on him being the main leader, I believe that today's church would realize the first century church had many leaders and not be so caught up in this idea that we all need to follow just one person. The Holy Spirit led the Church not man, it is the way it should have been because the Apostles did what Jesus told them to do.

I have heard it say that Paul was wrong in his thinking, and Peter made huge errors, and the other Apostles also could have done better, but what the teachers, who I will not name, have said this, fail to realize is that these were the Apostles sent out by Jesus, they did what they were told to do.

I have also heard it say by teachers that the Apostles basically walked on water like Jesus and knew everything that was happening and would happen in the future. Both of these extreme views in my opinion are wrong. The Apostles were just Israelite men of diverse backgrounds who were completely changed by a three year training time with Jesus and then an infilling of the Holy Spirit, who led them into their Ministry and gave them power they needed to walk the paths they needed to walk.

Peter did not have a relationship with scholarship, but instead with hardwork and catching fish. He was the perfect person to preach a life of service to people who looked toward the intelligentsia rather than common people. To quote an amazing scripture, "God has chosen the foolish things of the World to confound the wise".

Peter probably was one of the people this verse was referring to, he never would have gained traction amidst the Jewish Intelligentsia of his day because he didn't have a name, or the pedigree yet he did because he was the called out Apostle to the Jews.

Our famous Apostle has been made out to be hero, then villain, then hero again. I think in the Scriptures we see he was following what he knew. His responses in the Gospels, and then in his own writings, fit a certain psychological profile he would have acquired through waking up at 2 or 3 am to tend the nets, pull in the catch, clean the fish, then turn in before sundown worn out and tired. He was a man of sparse book learning, but quick decision making, when he thought something was good he said it, this is how most people who work with their hands are like.

In the trades, whether carpentry, ditch-digging, or fishing, you cannot question. Scholarly questions very rarely arise in learning a trade. First, a tradesman becomes an apprentice and learns the tools of the trade, and then the apprentice practice's what has been learned until the skills of a master are acquired.

After learning there is no why questions, the worker only has to work the craft. Peter exemplified this approach, in Preaching, Teaching, and how he responded to what the Holy Spirit required of him. He made mistakes while learning but after learning the craft just did what he learned, the Apostle Peter was truly the Rock Jesus referred to him. He was a man who you could depend on, once he figured something out there was no moving him from that conviction.

In those days in the fishing industry, a lot depended on how many boats a family had in the water to see how affluent the family was. Sometimes, the families sold their catch to village middlemen and went home after fishing; these were usually the poorer fisherman. Other families sold their own fish in the various markets themselves, making them the higher paid fisherman families.

Galilee was one of the most prosperous fishing areas in Israel. Recent archaeological evidence suggests that the dried fish from this area was bought and sold as far as Babylon. It was a good income for Simon Peter and his new family, but plenty of hardwork. What is quite amazing is that the same fish being caught there now are the ones Jesus ate; the fish are called Tilapia in North America, a fish common to most people today because of places like Walmart, Costco, and various food chains who sell this fish. Sometimes we think we are ahead of the people back then when in reality we are the same as those people.

Peter was married, and had a family when he went to preach the Gospel. Paul says as much in 1 Corinthians 9: 5. All of us, no matter how much academia we have or do not have, are shaped by where we are from. Peter and the other Apostles were no exception to this rule. Jesus probably taught the Apostles their Hebrew letters, except for maybe Matthew who was a tax collector which means he would have already knew them, but knowing your letters and being a scholar are very different.

Jesus was the Disciples Rabbi or teacher, and they were his disciples or Talmid. This meant that he taught them how to read the Torah Scrolls, how to recite the daily prayers in Hebrew if they hadn't already known, and he also taught them the basics of the Talmud or the Oral Torah rules.

In today's world the Torah Observant Jewish people start their children learning the Talmud and Torah at three years old, back then we do not yet know exactly how the people were taught, but we do know that Hebrew was spoken and the Torah Scrolls were read on a Triennial Cycle as it is today.

Jesus was a Scholar because he not only was able to read, but also hold the Torah Scroll, and also teach directly from it, meaning he knew the passages which were being read. It was very difficult to hold the Torah scroll because of their weight. If you did not do it properly you could damage the scroll and that was a very costly mistake.

The reason we know this is He always entered the Synagogues of the day to read from the Torah Scroll. The Torah Scrolls back then were so valuable that for an outsider to have been able to read from it meant that they were considered a Scholar, which means Jesus, had some sort of authoritative credentials.

Here is the passage in In Luke 4:14-22 *[14]Jesus returned to Galilee in the power of the Spirit, and news about him spread through the whole countryside.[15]**He was teaching in their synagogues, and everyone praised him**.*

*[16]He went to Nazareth, where he had been brought up, and on the Sabbath day he went into the synagogue, as was his custom. He stood up to read,[17]and the scroll of the prophet Isaiah was handed to him. **Unrolling it, he found the place where it is written:***

*[18]"The Spirit of the Lord is on me, because he has anointed me to proclaim good news to the poor. He has sent me to proclaim freedom for the prisoners and recovery of sight for the blind, to set the oppressed free,[19]to proclaim the year of the Lord's favor."*

*[20]**Then he rolled up the scroll, gave it back to the attendant and sat down**. The eyes of everyone in the synagogue were fastened on him.[21]He began by saying to them, "Today this scripture is fulfilled in your hearing."*

*²²All spoke well of him and were amazed at the gracious words*

*that came from his lips.*

Israel has had for 3,200 years a custom of reading the Torah aloud. They say this was started by Moses when he read the Torah aloud to the Israelites after receiving it from God on Mt Sinai. Ezra read it aloud as well after the first exile, and is said in the Talmud to have broken the Torah into 155 sections for a triennial cycle of readings which was set up 1200 years before Jesus' day. In Jesus' time the reading schedule they used was the one Ezra introduced, we do not know how it was broken down specifically but suffice it to say Jesus would have followed this schedule and taught His Disciples accordingly.

Today, the Torah is broken into 54 different parts and read in one year, this started in the beginning of the Diaspora when the Jewish Sages were in the province of Babylon. This is important to understand because the Jewish world ran on these Torah Portion reading schedules, they do today as well but it is not as evident as it was then. Peter would have known about this structure and used it in his own Ministry.

Christian Scholars always keep this information out of their commentaries for some reason, but the Disciples were with Jesus for 3 years constantly praying, studying, or listening to His messages. They wouldn't have learned as much as Paul did, or the Pharisees, who studied their whole life, but they became well acquainted with a normal Rabbinical world view in the 3 years Jesus was with them.

In 2 Peter 1:20, Peter explained a little bit of how he believed Scripture should be interpreted, this was what Jesus would have taught him. He writes that no one man can interpret Scripture by themselves. He says, and I am paraphrasing here; "no one can interpret their own way". He states in verse 21 that "no one could begin to understand the depths of the Fathers meaning of the Scriptures."

Earlier in the letter, in verse 16 he, again my paraphrase, explains how the Scripture he was involved in creating, didn't come from him, but from the Originator, which is the God of All Creation. This is very important to understand in relation to how Peter viewed the Scriptures, which was radically different than how we as 21<sup>st</sup> Century Believers view it.

For the past 1500 years, give or take, we have only had one perspective of interpreting Scripture, this has been from a decidedly Greek (or Hellenistic) perspective. Peter here seems to be saying that he interpreted scripture in a decidedly 1<sup>st</sup> Century Judaic way, in the next chapter I will explain why this way of interpreting Scripture is more similar to Judaic than Greek.

Peter also pointed to the Apostle Paul and encouraged his readers to (2 Peter 3:15-16) read his writings and not distort their meanings as some were doing. Paul was part of the Intelligentsia and would have been listened to had he been called to preach the Gospel to Israel, but he was called to the Gentiles. These things are very important to understand for all believers not just the people in leadership. In the next chapter we will continue our discussion on Peter's view of Scripture Interpretation, Paul's view, and then the Platonic view we are holding to in our day and age.

# Chapter 5

## Were the Apostles Rabbis or Philosophers?

*2 Peter 1:12-21, "*[12]* So I will always remind you of these things, even though you know them and are firmly established in the truth you now have. *[13]* I think it is right to refresh your memory as long as I live in the tent of this body, *[14]* because I know that I will soon put it aside, as our Lord Jesus Christ has made clear to me. *[15]* And I will make every effort to see that after my departure you will always be able to remember these things.*

*[16]* **For we did not follow cleverly devised stories when we told you about the coming of our Lord Jesus Christ in power, but we were eyewitnesses of his majesty.** *[17]* He received honor and glory from God the Father when the voice came to him from the Majestic Glory, saying, "This is my Son, whom I love; with him I am well pleased." *[18]* We ourselves heard this voice that came from heaven when we were with him on the sacred mountain.*

*[19] We also have the prophetic message as something completely reliable, and you will do well to pay attention to it, as to a light shining in a dark place, until the day dawns and the morning star rises in your hearts. [20] Above all, you must understand that no prophecy of Scripture came about by the prophet's own interpretation of things. [21] For prophecy never had its origin in the human will, but prophets, though human, spoke from God as they were carried along by the Holy Spirit."*

This passage gives us a glimpse into how the Apostles read, studied, and understood Scripture. Peter explains that Scripture is not understood by clever stories or private interpretation, my paraphrase. This general thinking is in complete accordance with how the Schools of Shammai and Hillel would have understood how to interpret Scripture.

There are many Denominations who have taken this verse Peter wrote, in only the literal sense of the meaning, which is the Peshat level according to Judaic Scholars. Now some may have a problem with my thoughts on this. If you are one of those people then all I can say is look at the writer, the timeframe he was writing in, and the audience he was writing to.

Peter was an Israeli who ascribed to a clear Pharisaical (which means Orthodox for today's Jews) way of living and understanding of the Bible and its teachings. When we see Peter and the other Apostles views on Scripture, as he is speaking about in this passage, we can clearly see he didn't follow a Sadducee interpretation, a Herodians view, nor did he follow a Hellenistic or Greek way of thinking. His thoughts are within the Pharisee methods of life and understanding. Hopefully as a Church we can at least agree on this premise. Below I will explain the main groups which were within Israel during the Apostles time.

1. **Pharisees-**

*The Pharisees formed a league or brotherhood of their own ("haburah"), admitting only those who, in the presence of three members, pledged themselves to the strict observance of Levitical purity, to the avoidance of closer association with the 'Am ha-Arez (the ignorant and careless boor), to the scrupulous payment of tithes and other imposts due to the priest, the Levite, and the poor, and to a conscientious regard for vows and for other people's property (Dem. ii.*

*3; Tosef., Dem. ii. 1). They called their members "ḥaberim" (brothers), while they passed under the name of "Perishaya," or "Perushim.".*

*The very institution of the synagogue for common worship and instruction was a Pharisaic declaration of the principle that the Torah is "the inheritance of the congregation of Jacob" (Deut. xxxiii. 3, Hebr.).*

*In establishing schools and synagogues everywhere and enjoining each father to see that his son was instructed in the Law (Yer. Ket. vii. 32c; Ḳid. 29a; Sifre, Deut. 46), the Pharisees made the Torah a power for the education of the Jewish people all over the world, a power whose influence, in fact, was felt even outside of the Jewish race (see R.Meïr in Sifra, Aḥare Mot, 13; Matt. xxiii. 15; comp. Gen. R. xxviii.; Jellinek, "B. H." vi., p. xlvi.).*

*The same sanctity that the priests in the Temple claimed for their meals, at which they gathered with the recitation of benedictions (I Sam. ix. 13) and after ablutions, the Pharisees established for their meals, which were partaken of in holy assemblies after purifications and amidst benedictions (Geiger, "Urschrift," pp. 121-124).*

*Especially were the Sabbath and holy days made the means of sanctification, and, as at the sacrifices, wine was used in honor of the day. A true Pharisee observed the same degree of purity in his daily meals as did the priest in the Temple (Tosef., Dem. ii. 2; so did Abraham, according to B. M. 87a), wherefore it was necessary that he should avoid contact with the 'am ha-arez (Ḥag. ii. 7).*

*(**Excerpt from the Jewish Encyclopedia on Pharisees**)*

## 2. Sadducees-

Mainly these were 1st Century Jewish elitists who wanted to maintain the priestly caste, but they were also liberal in their willingness to incorporate Hellenism into their lives, something the Pharisees opposed.

The Sadducees rejected the idea of the Oral Law and insisted on a literal interpretation of the Written Law; consequently, they did not believe in an afterlife, since it is not mentioned in the Torah. The main focus of Sadducee life was rituals associated with the Temple.

The Sadducees disappeared around 70 A.D., after the destruction of the Second Temple. None of the writings of the Sadducees has survived, so the little we know about them comes from their Pharisaic opponents, the whole picture of them cannot be seen.

These two "parties" served in the Great Sanhedrin, a kind of Jewish Supreme Court made up of 71 members whose responsibility was to interpret civil and religious laws.

The Karaites are said to be the nearest Sect of Israel closest to the Sadducees of the 1st Century, although if you compare them to how the Orthodox Jews explain the Sadducees you see many differences.

3. **Herodians**- Matthew 23:16-17 states

*16 They sent their disciples to him **along with the Herodians.**
"Teacher," they said, "we know that you are a man of integrity and that you teach the way of God in accordance with the truth. You aren't swayed by others, because you pay no attention to who they are. 17 Tell us then, what is your opinion? Is it right to pay the imperial tax to Caesar or not?"*

The Herodians really are not spoken about in history except for some blurbs about Herod's soldiers who may have belonged to the Party of Herod, spoken of in a political sense.

The common Scholarly position on the Herodians is that they were the political Party which sided with King Herod and his family.

Christian Commentators have written many things about them but they all start and end with theories, which are ok but do not give a solid basis to work from. What is seen in the passage above is some ideas to who the Herodians were, but again not fact, the only thing we can honestly say is that there were Herodians and because of the name they carried out King Herod's wishes.

## 4.  Essenes-

*"Essæi": Essenes =, "the modest," "humble," or "pious ones" [so Josephus in most passages; Pliny, in "Historia Naturalis," v. 17, used "Esseni"];A branch of the Pharisees who conformed to the most rigid rules of Levitical purity while aspiring to the highest degree of holiness.*

*They lived solely by the work of their hands and in a state of communism, devoted their time to study and devotion and to the practise of benevolence, and refrained as far as feasible from conjugal intercourse and sensual pleasures, in order to be initiated into the highest mysteries of heaven and cause the expected Messianic time to come ('Ab. Zarah ix. 15; Luke ii. 25, 38; xxiii. 51).*

*The strangest reports were spread about this mysterious class of Jews. Pliny (l.c.), speaking of the Essene community in the neighborhood of the Dead Sea, calls it the marvel of the world, and characterizes it as a race continuing its existence for thousands of centuries without either wives and children, or money for support, and with only the palm-trees for companions in its retreat from the storms of the world.*

*Philo, who calls the Essenes "the holy ones," after the Greek ὅσιοι, says in one place (as quoted by Eusebius, "Præparatio Evangelica," viii. 11) that ten thousand of them had been initiated by Moses into the mysteries of the sect, which, consisting of men of advanced years having neither wives nor children, practised the virtues of love and holiness and inhabited many cities and villages of Judea, living in communism as tillers of the soil or as mechanics according to common rules of simplicity and abstinence.*

*In another passage ("Quod Omnis Probus Liber," 12 et seq.) he speaks of only four thousand Essenes, who lived as farmers and artisans apart from the cities and in a perfect state of communism, and who condemned slavery, avoided sacrifice, abstained from swearing, strove for holiness, and were particularly scrupulous regarding the Sabbath, which day was devoted to the reading and allegorical interpretation of the Law. Josephus ("Ant." xv. 10, § 4; xviii. 1, § 5; "B.*

*J." ii. 8, §§ 2-13) describes them partly as a philosophical school like the Pythagoreans, and mystifies the reader by representing them as a kind of monastic order with semi-pagan rites.*

*Accordingly, the strangest theories have been advanced by non-Jewish writers, men like Zeller, Hilgenfeld, and Schürer, who found in Essenism a mixture of Jewish and pagan ideas and customs, taking it for granted that a class of Jews of this kind could have existed for centuries without leaving a trace in rabbinical literature, and, besides, ignoring the fact that Josephus describes the Pharisees and Sadducees also as philosophical schools after Greek models.*

**(Excerpt from the Jewish Encyclopedia on Essenes)**

## 5.   Hellenistic Jews-

Acts 6:1-2- *In those days when the number of disciples was increasing, the Hellenistic Jews among them complained against the Hebraic Jews because their widows were being overlooked in the daily distribution of food.*

Hellenism simply means imitation of the Greek culture, or as some Christian Scholars say, knowing the Greek Language. The second definition I personally have a problem with because it is too simple.

Hellenism of the Jews began when they began to live throughout the Roman Empire for trade. They needed to learn the customs, the language, and culture of the Greeks to be successful. Then Ptolemy II decided he would commission 71 Scholars of the Torah to make a Greek version of the Scriptures.

Every Scholar had to enter a room by himself and translate the Bible with no outside help or collaboration with the other Scholars. What emerged were 71 identical translations in Greek, this started the Jews, and Christians after them to accept what became known as the Septuagint (means 70). This translation changed the landscape of the Jewish Philosophical views within the Empire because the Jews could explain in the Greek language their history, culture, and beliefs.

These three groups were the main ones in the 1st Century Province of Israel. The only group remaining from these are the Pharisees, who have become the Orthodox Jews of Judaism. I will now try to very simply explain the Jewish way of bible interpretation. This interpretive system is called PaRDeS by Jewish Scholars. The word PaRDeS is an acronym for;

- P=Peshat (Literal Meaning),

- R=Remez (Hinted meaning, or implied meaning),

- D=Drash (Midrash or Sermon meaning of text or Word),

- S=Sod or Sud (Mystical or Heavenly meaning of text)

The first level of interpretation as stated earlier is the Peshat level or literal meaning of the scripture, then there is the Remez, which means what the scripture hints at or implies, then there is the Drash level which is the sermon or guideline understanding of the Scripture, and finally there is the Sod level which is the hidden level of spiritual understanding.

Within these levels there are methods on how to come to the proper understanding, this is what the schools of Hillel and Shammai taught their Disciples. Jesus also would have used these methods to teach His Disciples as it is the system which was common for teachers in Israel to employ. Most of us do not think about what the Disciples did in their three year tour with Jesus, but there were set rules in Israel for Disciples and Teachers.

It's important to recognize that Peter the Apostle was reinforcing this system of interpretation, in his reference of how to interpret Scripture. His hearers would have seen these references right away and knew what was meant, because we are so far removed and bombarded with another system of explanation it's hard for us to see his real meaning here, even though it is very simple. It's important to see that the Apostles understood and used this stringent system of rules to interpret even their own Scripture making.

Peter said in 2 Peter 1:20 that even the Prophet could not interpret what words he wrote. This understanding is properly explained by a purported argument between two Judaic Sages of the Second Temple Era.

*[An oven] that was cut into parts and sand was placed between the parts, Rabbi Eliezer maintained that it is pure (i.e., not susceptible to ritual impurity). The other sages said that it is susceptible to ritual impurity....On that day, Rabbi Eliezer brought them all sorts of proofs, but they were rejected.*

*Said he to them: "If the law is as I say, may the carob tree prove it." The carob tree was uprooted from its place a distance of 100 cubits.*

*Others say, 400 cubits. Said they to him: "One cannot prove*

*anything from a carob tree."*

*Said [Rabbi Eliezer] to them: "If the law is as I say, may*

*the aqueduct prove it." The water in the aqueduct began to flow*

*backwards. Said they to him: "One cannot prove anything from an*

*aqueduct."*

*Said he to them: "If the law is as I say, then may the walls*

*of the house of study prove it." The walls of the house of study*

*began to cave in.*

*Rabbi Joshua rebuked the walls by saying, "If Torah*

*scholars are debating a point of Jewish law, what are your*

*qualifications to intervene?" The walls did not fall, in deference to*

*Rabbi Joshua, nor did they straighten up, in deference to Rabbi*

*Eliezer. They still stand there at a slant.*

*Said he to them: "If the law is as I say, may it be proven*

*from heaven!" There then issued a heavenly voice which*

*proclaimed: "What do you want of Rabbi Eliezer -- the law is as he*

*says..."*

*Rabbi Joshua stood on his feet and said: "'The Torah is*

*not in heaven!" ... We take no notice of heavenly voices, since You,*

*G-d, have already, at Sinai, written in the Torah to "follow the*

*majority."*

Their explanation for not accepting the one man's belief could be spoken of this way, "We understand that heaven is on your side, we understand that the Earth is on your side, but we will trust the structure God has put into place and believe the majority."

Peter is basically saying the same thing. His premise is that the writers of Jesus' sayings did not add to the stories of Jesus, but recorded what they saw and heard. This is what the Prophets had done. He then explains that the Prophets were only speaking the Words of God as the Holy Spirit revealed it to them.

This is needed to be thought about in these days of knowledge explosion. There has been a path of Interpretative truth for over 4,000 years now and I believe we as the Church need to get back to that path of Interpretation in order to be on the solid foundations of faith the Apostles have given us through their writings.

Paul seemed to echo these sentiments when he said, "But even if we or an angel from heaven should preach a gospel other than the one we preached to you, let them be under God's curse!"

Gal. 1:8. This seems to mean that Paul also believed in the standard of corporate understanding in deriving at truth.

Remember when Paul and Barnabas were dispatched to Jerusalem to see if the group which came from Jerusalem and was preaching a different Gospel to the Gentiles then they preached was in error or not. The Jerusalem Church had to decide which was valid because it was different than what the Believers of Antioch were preaching.

The Apostle Paul submitted to the structure that the sages of the story argued about and delivered the letter as he was instructed to do. Acts 15 is a picture of how the Jewish people decided what was proper doctrine to follow and what was not. They went about it in a dual way, they prayed for guidance, then used the Torah principles handed down through the ages to decide what judgment was needed. In the next chapter we will look at the Churches beginnings.

# Chapter 6

# Was the Church meant to be a Kingdom?

Acts 15:1-34, *"Certain people came down from Judea to Antioch and were teaching the believers: "Unless you are circumcised, according to the custom taught by Moses, you cannot be saved." ² This brought Paul and Barnabas into sharp dispute and debate with them. So Paul and Barnabas were appointed, along with some other believers, to go up to Jerusalem to see the apostles and elders about this question.³ The church sent them on their way, and as they traveled through Phoenicia and Samaria, they told how the Gentiles had been converted. This news made all the believers very glad. ⁴ When they came to Jerusalem, they were welcomed by the church and the apostles and elders, to whom they reported everything God had done through them.*

*⁵ Then some of the believers who belonged to the party of the Pharisees stood up and said, "The Gentiles must be circumcised and required to keep the law of Moses."*

*⁶ The apostles and elders met to consider this question. ⁷ After much discussion, Peter got up and addressed them: "Brothers, you know that some time ago God made a choice among you that the Gentiles might hear from my lips the message of the gospel and believe. ⁸ God, who knows the heart, showed that he accepted them by giving the Holy Spirit to them, just as he did to us. ⁹ He did not discriminate between us and them, for he purified their hearts by faith. ¹⁰ Now then, why do you try to test God by putting on the necks of Gentiles a yoke that neither we nor our ancestors have been able to bear? ¹¹ No! We believe it is through the grace of our Lord Jesus that we are saved, just as they are."*

*¹² The whole assembly became silent as they listened to Barnabas and Paul telling about the signs and wonders God had done among the Gentiles through them. ¹³ When they finished, James spoke up. "Brothers," he said, "listen to me. ¹⁴ Simon has described to us how God first intervened to choose a people for his name from the Gentiles. ¹⁵ The words of the prophets are in agreement with this, as it is written:*

*¹⁶ " 'After this I will return and rebuild David's fallen tent. Its ruins I will rebuild, and I will restore it,¹⁷ that the rest of mankind may seek the Lord, even all the Gentiles who bear my name, says the Lord, who does these things'—¹⁸ things known from long ago.*

*¹⁹ "It is my judgment, therefore, that we should not make it difficult for the Gentiles who are turning to God. ²⁰ Instead we should write to them, telling them to abstain from food polluted by idols, from sexual immorality, from the meat of strangled animals and from blood. [21] For the law of Moses has been preached in every city from the earliest times and is read in the synagogues on every Sabbath.*

*[22] Then the apostles and elders, with the whole church, decided to choose some of their own men and send them to Antioch with Paul and Barnabas. They chose Judas (called Barsabbas) and Silas, men who were leaders among the believers. [23] With them they sent the following letter:*

*The apostles and elders, your brothers,*

*To the Gentile believers in Antioch, Syria and Cilicia:*

*Greetings.*

*[24] We have heard that some went out from us without our authorization and disturbed you, troubling your minds by what they said. [25] So we all agreed to choose some men and send them to you with our dear friends Barnabas and Paul— [26] men who have risked their lives for the name of our Lord Jesus Christ. [27] Therefore we are sending Judas and Silas to confirm by word of mouth what we are writing. [28] It seemed good to the Holy Spirit and to us not to burden you with anything beyond the following requirements: [29] **You are to abstain from food sacrificed to idols, from blood, from the meat of strangled animals and from sexual immorality.** You will do well to avoid these things.*

*Farewell.*

*<sup>30</sup> So the men were sent off and went down to Antioch, where they gathered the church together and delivered the letter. <sup>31</sup> The people read it and were glad for its encouraging message. <sup>32</sup> Judas and Silas, who themselves were prophets, said much to encourage and strengthen the believers. <sup>33</sup> After spending some time there, they were sent off by the believers with the blessing of peace to return to those who had sent them. <sup>[34]</sup> <sup>35</sup> But Paul and Barnabas remained in Antioch, where they and many others taught and preached the word of the Lord."*

I know it was a long passage but I think to properly understand certain truths of the Scriptures we needed whole passages, not one or two verses. The Elders, Apostles, and other leaders of the newly formed Church met together to hear the dispute over what truly constituted the Gospel message for the gentiles, then after the arguments they had to make a judgement on it. The discussions of the Apostles and Elders were not written down unfortunately.

The context of arguments were not given precisely, but enough understanding is given to see that much of what was used as evidence for one side or the other, was Jesus' teachings, and the common understanding of Prophetic teachings handed down by the Pharisaical tradition. In the edict the Apostles and Elders handed down in Acts 15:22-35, it was almost identical to what the Rabbis of today refer to as the Noahide Laws. Is this a coincidence? I do not believe it is.

This part of Scripture alone should prove to most people that the Apostles and first Leaders of the Church were following a Judaic system, and more specifically a Pharisaical mode of interpretation and mode of belief.

According to the Rabbis of that day and today, the Noahide Laws govern what Gentiles need to do if they want to follow God, these are the laws the Leaders of the Church told the Gentiles to do. I have highlighted the Noahide laws in the text at the beginning of this chapter.

The Rabbis of then and today realized the Torah laws are mainly directed to Israelites, but also realize that Gentiles will be drawn to the Torah and God, and had to see what rules they needed to follow. The way the Apostles and Leaders dealt with problems shows that in the Apostles minds they believed that the physical Kingdom was already established by God and was Israel, not the sect of Judaism they were starting.

Interesting to see as well, the judgment was pronounced by James, Jesus' Brother, who after hearing what the Apostles, Elders, and other leaders discussed had the responsibility to decide the course of action for the newly formed Church. It wasn't Peter, Andrew, John or his brother James.

James the brother of Jesus, who one 1$^{st}$ Century historian (Hegesippus) said was a Nazarene from birth, was the head of the Jerusalem Church and made the judgment. This is another example of a Judaic way of dealing with problems.

Some churches (mainly the Catholic Church) try to say that this James was only a cousin of Jesus and point to the fact that at Jesus' death on the Cross he seemed to ask John to take care of His Mother.

The churches who teach this version of the story say this was an old Hebrew custom which shows that Mary, Jesus' Mother, had no other family to take care of her. Most scholars have shown this type of thinking to be wrong, so I will not spend too much time on it.

This 'understanding' however opens many questions but I will limit it to two.

1. If Jesus was an only son, and Mary never had other children, wouldn't the cousins take care of his mother without being asked?

2. My second question is, if the bible clearly states that James made the decision of what to send as judgment, and Paul states in I Cor. 15:7 Jesus specifically appeared to James, and James was spoken of by many historians (Hegesippus, Eusebius, and Josephus), as the leader of the Church, why would Jesus ask John (his cousin according to church tradition), to do this instead of James who was with Mary early in Mark 3:31?

I believe that Jesus was trying to be good to his mother, and let her be taken care of by someone who would outlive her. Jesus was not only the Messiah but also a Prophet who would have known the future of each of his brothers and Apostles. It could be just as simple as that.

It could also mean that because John was the only male there he had to ask someone, so he asked John, and it was recorded to show that Jesus cared for his family. This is only my wild speculation of course, but everyone can have opinions.

Let's explore for a little bit the difference between Judaic and Platonic systems of understanding to see how a physical kingdom belief may have crept into the church once the Apostles were not on the Earth anymore to refute it.

The Judaic way of understanding begins and ends with the Scriptures interpreted by what is called the Talmud, or Oral Torah. The Oral Torah is presented 2 ways, one a more conservative view by the Orthodox, and another more Liberal view by the Reformed Jews.

The Rabbis teach that unless student learns the Talmud he/she cannot believe what is proper about life. The Orthodox Jews believe the Talmud or Oral Torah was handed down by Moses, because he received it from God on Mt Sinai. It was then given to the Leaders of each Tribe who formed the Sanhedrin (or council of Elders, Numbers 11:6), they then handed it down through the Sanhedrin orally to succeeding generations, until it was codified in the Second Century. They believe that the laws handed down are binding, and when Jews study it will receive blessings in accordance with their belief of the words of the Talmud.

The more Liberal way of looking at the Talmud or Oral Torah, loosely states that it is an ancient philosophical way to interpret the Torah which Moses gave to the Israel Nation after his 40 days on Mt Sinai. The reformed Jews also do not find the Talmud to be binding laws but suggestions of how the ancients viewed the Torah during their Cultural times and hint at what the proper application could mean in the present time.

These are both simplistic explanations of how the Jews view the Talmud, but again we can spend many chapters on the discussions of these things but that is not what we are looking at, we are looking at whether or not the Church was to be a physical Kingdom, or just a belief system.

Either one of these ways of looking at the Talmud is valid in my opinion, and a combination of the two are probably the correct path, but the key here is to see that Israel puts the Oral Torah or

Talmud on a level plane with Scripture, thus making its decrees very important for every person who accepts and follows Torah.

We will look at the Talmud a little more to see how the 1st Century Jews viewed their understanding of how to interpret the Torah. Jewish scholars of the past 1000 years have taught that the Mishnah was first organized into a written document by Rabban Gamaliel II's (incidentally Paul's Teacher) son, Rabbi Judah the Prince.

He took all the different headings of the Oral Law and organized them into one treatise called the Mishnah Torah (literally Oral Law). Rabbi Judah the Prince was the head of the Sanhedrin in those days. He published this Mishnah Torah around 200AD.

The Jewish scholars of that day realized they were in a time of relative calm after the destruction of the Temple, and felt compelled to make a record for posterity of what they did while in Israel. They knew they were facing a long exile from their Temple and Israel, and sought to write down the proper way to believe, which was the most important part of their lives in this time.

The Gemara (or discussions of Torah), took another 300 years to write down, but when finished these two documents together make up the Oral Torah, which became known as the Talmud. Today there are many different translations for English, French, German, Dutch, Russian, and Arabic that is all that I know. I have heard there are a total of nine translations, but haven't seen any others than these. We live in amazing times when we can read this amazing ancient doctrine in our own language.

Rabbi Judah the Prince, say the Jewish scholars of today, protected the Jewish culture by creating a living document rather than a mausoleum of a dead past. I heartily agree because without the Talmud, the tribe of Judah (the Jews) would never have been able to keep their culture, teachings, or perspective on life alive without it.

What is important to see is that the Jews believe the Talmud is a living document which receives life into it when each and every generation of Torah Observant people breathes life into it, by doing what it says.

The Jew has fiercely defended this Oral Law. Sometimes being burned at the stake for its truths, other times being cast into deserts to die, or sent to live in desolate places. The Jews have been sent to be eaten by animals, or killed by mass murder. They always kept its secrets, and followed its precepts no matter the personal cost. If you read any of the Holocaust stories you will see within the people who suffered there, an ability to endure because of the Talmudic stories, wisdom, and logical belief it imparted to the victims.

The Oral Law had never been in print like it is today; we are truly blessed to be able to not only read the documents, but also to hear teachings from our Jewish Brothers from it.

The devotion to the Oral Torah has been at the bottom of the desire of Israel to recover the texts the Roman Catholic Church stole and locked up in their archives. The Christian Church has continually persecuted the Jews, not from their belief in the Torah, but because of their devotion to the Oral Torah's logic and belief system.

This for me has been a very hard history to look into, but one I challenge every Disciple of the Lord to engage in, because without seeing the Talmud for what it is, we cannot fully understand what Jesus and the Apostles taught.

The main point to realize is that this Talmudic discourse is what the Apostles engaged in with the Pharisees. It's true that the Talmud was not written yet when the Apostles were around, but from the time of Hillel before Jesus, to Rabbi Judah the Prince, to the Rabbis who wrote the Gemara, to today's Orthodox Rabbis, all have used the Talmudic logic of discussion and teaching style.

Jesus used this type of logic when he discussed what was proper and what was not proper. We as His Body had lost this type of thinking, but now the Lord is bringing it back into the church, and for this I am very grateful, because it is how Paul, Peter, James, John and the other Apostles would have talked and how they would have taught their Disciples.

In contrast to Judaic thinking which begins and ends with the philosophical construct handed down in the Talmud, Platonic or Greek thinking begins by looking at the empirical facts of the core sciences, Mathematics, Astronomy, Geometry, and Music, without a preconceived structure of philosophy for guidance.

These sciences have not really changed since Plato's time. The only difference is today we would not lump music into the core, but I think we are mistaken, as music is definitely something of a core science to human beings and should be given an equal part of understanding.

Plato believed that before a student can properly become acquainted with Philosophy, the student needed to have a foundation of facts with which to make Philosophical assumptions. Sound familiar?

Rabbis however, teach that the first thing a student should learn about is the Torah, written and Oral. The readers who believe Torah means Jewish law, I would remind them it actually means teachings of righteousness or the first five books of the Hebrew or Old Testament Scriptures.

The Rabbi's, dating back to Hillel and Shammai, two generations before Jesus, instituted a strict set of rules for teaching students the philosophy of Torah first before the sciences. This differed drastically with Plato, although some

Scholars of today want to say that the Sages of Judaism and Plato had much in common with respect to philosophy. I only agree they were of the same type of scholar (brilliant and innovative), but had drastic differences with the applications and meanings of their philosophy of teaching.

The Sages taught that students needed to have a foundation of Torah Study in order to understand. Plato would have considered it dangerous to study philosophy first before knowing the empirical facts of life. In today's society most parents say, I want my child to make up his own mind after he has all the facts. This is an echo of Platonic thought; it runs deep in a Westerners mind and heart.

The Rabbis would argue that unless that child has the wisdom of the Elders he cannot make the proper choice with the facts. The Greek thinker would say let the facts show the child the way. The argument is simple, do you want your child to learn about hard facts first with no understanding of how to interpret them, or do you want your child to learn how to interpret things first then learn the hard facts.

Plato said he wanted people to be free thinkers, this is a noble concept, but one I believe is difficult to achieve because of our penchant to do evil, and use the so-called facts to our own designs. Plato postulated that the facts will lead to their proper conclusions, my paraphrase, but in essence it is what we believe today in the West. He honestly wanted the people of Rome and its New Empire to be progressive thinkers and usher into the World a new age of peace and prosperity, he was a great man, and has done more than most in respect to educating people.

What has happened however, with getting the facts and nothing but the facts, is those facts have become their own truth. In his approach, what is forgotten is that being humans, we live half in a philosophical world because of our imagination, and half in an instinctual world because of our bodies, and are more led by our physical needs and desires than our minds and spirits. We cannot just automatically understand the facts which are around us without attaching philosophical underpinnings to those facts.

We as humans were designed with imagination and a brain which is not disciplined because of our desire to sin rather than do what is right. I think every parent sees this the first time they see their sweet innocent child in need of a lesson in manners. Children usually, do not instinctually realize they are not supposed to scream in a funeral, nor do they instinctually understand that sound travels, they need to realize that their actions cause others discomfort or joy. This understanding comes from a parent explaining to the child how life works. It is true that some children's personalities are introspective and they do not overstep the proper boundaries of social etiquette but listen to their parents and obey them with no questions, but most children in regards to proper social interaction need to learn a social philosophy before the facts of social interaction hurt them.

Children also do not play because they innately want to have fun; children play in order to understand their surroundings better. When fun and games become undisciplined is when we have allowed the child to figure things out for themselves, a good parent will not allow the child to go into a situation unprepared so they prepare them by the proper philosophy of interaction before they are in the situation.

We as humans naturally desire to know about things, but knowing and doing what is right are two different things. If a parent is not there to explain what each 'fact' a child finds out about truly is, the child will use those 'facts' in their own way, which most of the time is destructive.

As an example of this, our brains can make a cloud look like a cow, does this mean the cloud is a cow. No, this is just how we interpret what we see, which incidentally we need to do in order to see. If we look at the clouds as a computer would, with the actual physical properties, we miss the shapes, the beauty, or the destructive nature the clouds could be showing us.

Our senses tell us much more about clouds than just what they are. These senses need to have a prism of interpretation to properly understand what they are feeling. This interpretation is loosely called philosophy, and it underpins everything we see, touch, smell, and experience.

This is why in my personal opinion, it is so important to answer patiently our children's questions, no matter how many times they ask, because we need to allow a child to not only develop inquisitiveness, but also a desire for the answer.

If we do not share the answer then the child will make up their own and become disconnected from people, or the truth.

Some would say that philosophy clouds everyone's judgment and creates chaos. I believe that this type of philosophy is a short sighted view of things, and ends up as a chaotic worldview, because without a thought out intelligent philosophy, people will not look for answers to problems the facts show us. With a well thought out worldview, our brains will naturally work out problems and add to their worldview to encompass the new problems uncovered. Our brains are muscles ultimately, and when we only exercise one aspect of the muscle it suffers. Philosophy is a very important part of our brains training.

Many people believe if we leave philosophy out of science then we can better understand ourselves and the world we live in. As the example about clouds suggests, we need both, the real facts and a proper philosophical prism to understand them. Without one or the other we will get side tracked into believing a lie. You need both to have any type of stable society.

If you're a proponent of the Greek way of thinking then you will want to find out why you believe, before you believe. Greek belief begins with core sciences and ends with mysterious spirituality. The Greek way of thinking is summed up by this perspective,

*"Plato and Socrates believed true happiness can be found only in pursuing virtue and reason. They believed our soul must rule over our appetites and our desires. Socrates was on a quest for self-perfection. Plato thought of our physical world as a kind of shadow world, one that is a little bit real, but not ultimately real. The true philosopher was one who sought to understand the deeper nature of things and to not be satisfied with only a surface; superficial understanding of the nature of what is ultimately real."*

**Quote from Wikispaces**

Plato here is explaining that the natural realm is not real, but still needs to be understood because without this understanding you cannot go deeper. This philosophy when broken down into a belief system becomes something like this. First you need to understand the natural world (get the facts of the core sciences), then look into the philosophical beliefs of those facts, and finally come to your own conclusions of what the combination of the two parts (Core Sciences and Philosophy), means to you. Thus understanding what reality is.

If you're a Judaic minded person first you believe, then you find out why you believe it, then you choose whether to continue in belief or just live without any belief. Judaic belief begins and ends with doing. There is a collection of wisdom within Judaism called the Pirke Avot; it puts the Judaic perspective this way;

> *"The most important aspect in life is not study of Torah (or the Bible), but its practice."*

Hillel the Elder who started a school in Jerusalem which continues on today with the Orthodox Jews was known for two sayings,

> *"If I am not for myself, who will be for me? And when I am for myself, what am 'I'? And if not now, when? "and*
>
> *(2) the expression of the ethic of reciprocity, or "Golden Rule": "That which is hateful to you, do not do to your fellow. That is the whole Torah; the rest is the explanation; go and learn."*

I personally believe either path is ok to follow for Society. Greek thinking has been the Western mantra for over 2000 years and has worked well to build an exceptional society. Judaic thinking has been around for well over 5,000 years and has built, as well as safeguarded an impressive group of people called the Jews. When a society changes to meet new societal pressures, we need to ask which path is proper for us.

For the church, which philosophy should we stand in? I think this is the question we are asking ourselves right now. I have chosen to stand in a Judaic philosophy, does it make me a Jew, no. It makes me someone who realizes the Greek way of understanding is incompatible with living what I believe to be authentic Christian Faith.

# Chapter 7

# Was Origen a friend or a foe?

In this chapter I want to look into why the 3$^{rd}$ century church adopted a Greek philosophical approach to interpreting Scripture. It is very interesting to see that our 21$^{st}$ Century Church has little in common intellectually with the Apostles and their Disciples; we look much closer to Plato and the people who followed his rules of logic and thought. Why did the Church stop studying in a Judaic way and embrace Greek thinking?

There are many reasons the Church left the path of Judaic Interpretation, but when I look through the early church Fathers one person stands out to me far above anyone else. He loved an interpretive model called Allegorical Interpretation, and he used it from a decidedly Platonic way of thinking. Origen was his name, and he is very popular today with Theologians and would be theologians.

Within Greek Allegorical interpretation the most important part of interpretation comes from knowing the meaning of the word, in order to be able to make assumptions about what the text means, or may mean. Allegorical Interpretation from a Greek perspective seemed to be introduced by a Third Century Scholar named Origen.

He was a very pious believer, who (some scholars say) castrated himself because he read in the Gospel Matthew 19:12 that Jesus said if anything causes you to sin, cut it off. After he castrated himself he realized this was probably not how Jesus wanted His Words to be followed. He decided this teaching must mean something different.

He was right about it meaning something different than the literal interpretation he used, if he actually castrated himself as most scholars believe. He however chose to set aside the Hebraic or Rabbinic wisdom of understanding and instead to find meaning for these Scriptures through Greek or Neo-Platonic logic.

Origen talked about Scriptures this way;

*"Scripture contains three levels of meaning, corresponding to the threefold Pauline (and Platonic) division of a person into body, soul and spirit. The bodily*

*level of Scripture, the bare letter, is normally helpful as it stands to meet the needs of the more simple. The psychic level, corresponding to the soul, is for making progress in perfection. ... [The] spiritual interpretation deals with 'unspeakable mysteries' so as to make humanity a "partaker of all the doctrines of the Spirit's counsel"*

The model which Origen is introducing here was not accepted by the Leaders of his day, quite the contrary. The Church Leaders of his day condemned him. To be fair to Origen, some scholars suggest that the Leaders of his day could not have anything to do with him because if he had castrated himself it was a capital offense in the 3<sup>rd</sup> Century, and would have given Origen a bad name.

Regardless of why the leaders condemned him, they seemed to not accept his teachings, much more than not accepting him and his supposed offense against the State. When the 4<sup>th</sup> Century rolled around however, with leaders like Eusebius, Pamphilius, and others, Origen's writings found fertile soil in which to grow.

Origen used Platonic logic to explain the Soul, he failed to mention Paul called himself a Pharisee of Pharisee's, which means he never would have used a Platonic model to understand or teach Scripture. He was never a Hellenistic thinking Israeli, some in

Tarsus were when he was born there, but his father enrolled him in Gamaliel II's school when he was young, probably 3 or 4 years of age, so he would have grown up in Jerusalem under one of the pre-eminent teachers of Judaism, not only in his time but also still today within Judaism.

Here is Paul's description of who he is

Acts 22:3, *"I am a Jew, born in Tarsus of Cilicia, but brought up in this city. I studied under Gamaliel and was thoroughly trained in the law of our ancestors. I was just as zealous for God as any of you are today."*

There is a discussion about whether or not Paul was taught by Gamaliel II but I think Paul's writings are proof enough he was with this teacher. In the Jewish Encyclopedia they say that Gamaliel may have never taught publicly. I find this hard to believe because of the Honor that Gamaliel II was afforded, he is referred to as Rabban Gamaliel which means Master Teacher Gamaliel. The reason the Jewish people even discuss whether or not Gamaliel II taught publicly is because only the Gospels and the book of Acts says he does, so they try to stay away from supporting this idea because of the persecution they endured at the hands of the Church who supposedly follow Paul's teachings.

Paul would have used the model of interpretation handed down by Hillel the Great, who taught Gamaliel II's father, and subsequently him. Hillel the Great explained that there is a Soul and Body, and Spirit, but the body has not imprisoned the soul as Plato taught. Plato taught that the Soul was imprisoned by the body which was an adversary to the soul, which only wants to do good (this good is not defined by any ethical teachings only by the term good). Plato believed that the soul and body were separate entities at war with each other. This is what Origen taught to his Disciples.

Hillel explained by Scripture, that there is a Soul, Body, and Spirit (Nefesh=Instincts, Neshamah=Emotions, Ruah or Ruach=Intellect) but they are all one, and when the person follows Torah, can work in unison to serve God because this is what God intended.

Hillel used the Hebrew language to prove without a shadow of doubt that these three parts of a person is what God is struggling with us to follow His Path. The Torah principle Hillel used to understand this when he taught about the Soul comes from;

Genesis 6:1-3, *"When human beings began to increase in number on the earth and daughters were born to them,[2] the sons of God saw that the daughters of humans were beautiful, and they married any of them they chose. [3] Then the Lord said, "My Spirit will not contend with humans forever, for they are mortal; their days will be a hundred and twenty years."*

The Orthodox Jews of today have some amazing teachings on their concepts of the different levels of the Soul, how it was created, and why it is termed in their vernacular the 'Spark of Godliness in side of us'.

The basis for the second layer of teaching regarding the Soul is from verse three of Genesis 6. Before this verse, the soul began in Genesis 1 at Creation, then after the second layer of the Soul as explained above, Judaism teaches how the Soul allows us to love each other as ourselves, and how we love our neighbor as our self. I want to show you that the Judaic understanding seemingly states the same basic 3 part principle of Greek thinking in relation to the soul, but when you wade into the teaching deeper, it is not the same at all.

Linear logic, something that starts with a presupposition, usually based on meanings of words, and ends with a conclusion, is the Greek way of learning. Judaic logic in contrast, starts with a clear Torah premise or law (arrived at by God's Word or Rabbinic Decree), then intersects this Torah principle with all relevant teachings or knowledge and devises a way to live.

Within Greek logic everything is tightly and neatly wrapped up in a bow of linear logic and closed tightly. In Judaic thinking you have an unmovable premise, then look to see how it relates to real life before making a decree. This makes it a much more fluid in practice because the premise will always stay the same no matter the culture you're in.

This is ultimately a much better thought out system for belief, because the unmovable premise never can change, but how to live can. Within Greek thinking once the premise is proven wrong the whole belief system is proven false. As an example we can see how the Greek form of Capitalism has put Christianity into a box of democratic thought. It is difficult for Christianity to function within any other culture. Judaism however is more fluid and was able to prosper within Communism in Russia, Capitalism in the West, and even within the Old Persian and Babylon Nations they were in, because the adherents went with Torah principles not cultural norms. Most Western Christians find it very difficult to translate their worldview into other non-democratic Societies.

Origen tried to imply that Paul taught the same as Plato, but he needed to realize who Paul was. When we make claims about how someone thought, as I am, and what Origen did, we need to bring some solid evidence to back up our claims. Origen's only claim, from my reading of him anyway, is that because he thinks he has answered all the questions logically in his mind, he believes surely every other intelligent person would think like him.

I am not trying to say that Origen was bad; I think he was an honest Intellectual of his day, but unfortunately he believed Plato was better than the Jewish Sages like Hillel and Shammai, and used blanket statements to make Paul's statements seem like they came from a Greek logical structure rather than the over 1,000 year breadth of Judaic life and teachings.

Remember, when the Jews were liberated from Babylon and then Persia, they decided they needed to realize who they were as a people and come up with a clear way to live. From Nehemiah and Ezra's time the Pharisee movement had begun, so the Israelite had already spent much time studying Torah and living its principles.

For Origen to automatically assume, which he may not have done because he is not here to defend himself and there is no writings explaining why he chose platonic thought over Judaic, that Paul followed a Greek interpretation on the Soul, is somehow disingenuous of him and his scholarship.

The writings I have read has never explained why he thought Paul believed in Greek Logic over Judaic, most scholars take this to mean it was the assumption everyone had therefore the correct one, I believe after looking at Paul in context then comparing him with the Jewish writers of his day, he never believed in Greek Logic over Judaic.

The Bishop of Alexandria, when Origen wrote his first book, was Demetrius who had taught him in the now famed Alexandrian Catechetical School. Demetrius never ordained Origen as a Priest even though he was a very bright student.

Origen became ordained as a Priest, when he assumed the leadership role of the school for Demetrius, or when he traveled to Jerusalem to meet with some friends. Scholarship is divided on this, but regardless, whether by an act of his own authority or by the Bishop in Jerusalem named Alexander, it is not truly known, only that it angered Demetrius, and Origen was summarily dismissed by Demetrius for this. Eusebius and others, who were followers of Origen's teachings are the ones who wrote extensively about how Origen became Ordained, so it's difficult to believe their accounts are completely accurate and honest.

What Demetrius dismissal shows is that Origen was not a leader of his day, nor did he have the leaders who taught him blessings to become a leader. I believe he was dismissed because of what he taught, not who he was as some have taught.

Becoming a Priest, which wasn't really the term then, they used the term Bishop, was started after Constantine organized and structured the church by the Roman form of Government, meant something different than today.

The Church was still in the Jewish custom of handing down S'mikha or Ordination, which would have started with Jesus and the Apostles, and then carried on to Demetrius through his teacher, and then through Demetrius to his Disciples who he deemed worthy of being a leader. Demetrius would have had Ordained Origen as a leader if Origen would have been ready, but for some reason he never gave him Ordination.

Many scholars now and church Historians of the 4th Century want to spin Origen as an impulsive youth who reacted to things emotionally rather than going by the Leaders opinions and this was what made Demetrius not trust him. I would almost concur with these people; except the 4th Century leaders who say this were trying to lay a firm foundation of Hellenism for Christianity, something which I do not see is there. Origen tried unsuccessfully to convince his leaders of a new way to view the Scriptures and was rejected.

In my mind Origen was a dangerous person because he used his intellect to subvert the Churches way of interpreting the Scriptures. I think by comparing Origen's commentaries, to Clements of the 2nd Century, or Papias, or Polycarp, we see he made a subtle shift to Greek thinking. If nothing else he was not well received in his day by the leaders who knew him best.

He was well liked by the people according to letters of the time where he is mentioned. People saw him as an honest, humble, and almost too brilliant for his own good. Consequently, a rich benefactor named Ambrose paid for his books to be published and distributed. Eusebius was Bishop in Pamphilius, and used Origen's writings to teach in the Academy.

Origen was one of the first Intellectuals to break from Judaic understanding to Greek and caused a stir with his conclusions, because they differed from what was known to the leaders of the day. If you read him now, you will understand him much better than the Church of his own day did.

He was the first Christian writer to explain Neo-Platonic ideas, and use them to interpret the Gospels, Pauline Epistles, and other Apostolic Writings. He even 'fixed' what he said was problems with the Septuagint (Greek translation of the Old Testament), mainly in Daniel, and some Prophetic books.

He was thought to have been a Heretic by leaders like Demetrius, but what the leaders of the 4$^{th}$ Century, principally Eusebius, realized was he thought a bit deeper about how Greek Philosophy was a better fit for interpretation when read strictly from the Greek translation. Eusebius, I believe, realized he showed them how to change a Judaic concept like Abrahams Bosom into a Greek one of Hell, or change a Judaic concept of the Godhead, into one of separate but complete entities by using the Greek language rather than Hebrew. He wasn't a pagan; he just explained Biblical concepts with Greek Philosophy.

What is interesting is he was taught Hebrew from his father Leonidas, before his father was martyred, although this is not fully confirmed, and if you talk to two scholars you get ten valid opinions on this subject. He must have had to learn Hebrew in order to learn rabbinic teachings about the scriptures, but he rejected this Hebrew logic for the philosophy of Rome instead.

Today Origen is put on a pedestal as being the first true Theologian. He is seen as a man who was misunderstood because the Church was in its infancy. I believe he introduced a Greek way of thinking, which emptied the New Testament of its proper basis and replaced it with a philosophy which has nothing to do with how the Scriptures should have been interpreted. Demetrius and the other leaders of his day had it right when they tried to mute him, without his influence on the future church leaders I believe we would study the Scriptures radically different.

Many Scholars of today say in defense of Origen that he was one of the first true Intellectual who understood the full ramifications of Paul's new covenant teachings. These Scholars point to the supposed 'facts'.

The first fact they quote is that Paul used direct quotes from the Septuagint in his writings, which means according to their theory, that Paul accepted the Septuagint as Scripture, which makes him a Hellenist.

These scholars also say that Hellenist only referred to Jews who spoke Greek but not necessarily embraced Greek logic, unfortunately this does not line up with how the Jewish people think themselves.

It is true that some non-Hellenists learned Greek, as it was a means of communication with the Empire, but this was a very small number. The population of the Jews at this time was not big, so the number of Jews who would have needed to communicate with the Roman Prelates and Officials was small. Most Jews of the day spoke in Aramaic the common trade language and Hebrew for their religion. Most Judeans of the day would not have been able to write as this was left to a small number of scribes who had passed on knowledge of the Hebrew Script to their sons, or apprentices they chose to teach. People could read Hebrew but writing was different.

Jewish Historians of today (Berel Wein and others) believe the Hellenization of Israel in this period was what led to the problems of the Jewish Nations belief in the Torah. Non-karaite Jewish Historians teach that if a Jew was Hellenised it meant he read the Torah in Greek only, which the people of Israel would find abhorrent. Jewish historians also teach a Hellenised Jew of this generation would never have been respected by the Israeli. A Hellenised Jew could never enter into one of Israel's top Academies, especially Hillel's school to be taught by Gamaliel II.

The last and most damning lesson the Jewish Historians teach about the Hellenised Jew of this generation is that the Hellenised Jew would consider the Greek Philosophers as almost Jewish in thought. The argument goes then that Paul was probably never a student in Gamaliel II's school but only listened to his teachings in the Temple. This would not have been possible as to learn from Gamaliel II meant you had to be one of his Disciples (or Talmid) as even whether or not he taught publicly is being debated now by Jewish Scholars.

I have to bring up something now that people may not like, but it goes to our penchant as Christians, to misinterpret what the Pharisees actually believed. Christians of today have a wrong opinion about Hillel. I have heard many preachers say he was liberal, and they use it in a context of being liberal today. This is just absurd, Hillel was one of the more conservative, highest thinking Jewish Sages of all time. He is on par with Moses, Solomon, Ezra, Nehemiah, and even Jesus as a teacher.

As Believers, we think about Hillel's teachings almost every day, he is the one who first introduced the concept of how the Law is summed up with what Jesus said was "Love the Lord your God with all your heart, soul and mind, and love your neighbor as yourself." Jesus was speaking from Hillel's teaching, which was common in the academies of the day. Whether Jesus attended these academies, or whether he only knew this innately, is not really introduced to us from the Gospels. We surmise that Jesus came out of nowhere and then began calling Disciples to himself, then had a Province of Israel wide teaching ministry. I submit this wasn't the case, but do not have time in this book to explain the reasons I believe this.

Jesus also used Hillel's teachings on the resurrection of the body, a Messianic age, and allowing more freedoms to common people. Jesus only disagreed with Hillel in the matter of divorce, but Hillel was much stricter on divorce than people of today. I heard a well-known preacher say that Hillel allowed divorce for any reason for the man but none for the women. What this good hearted Preacher did not realize is divorce was set up to help the women not the man. Hillel's whole premise for teaching was to teach people not to destroy but to build up so the Messianic age could come.

It is true the women could not give the writ of divorce, which in today's vernacular means it was heavily weighted in the man's favor, but remember the women of this day had no rights at all. To give a writ of divorce meant there was no problems for the women to remarry, which was not the case if the man just left the women without the writ. Hillel tried to insist on giving a Writ of Divorce whenever a man left his wife, thus allowing her freedom to have a life.

Divorce was introduced as Jesus said, because of the hardening of the heart of the man, if the man was honest then it shouldn't have even been needed, but in that society, just like it was in ours 40 years ago, women were stuck in wrong relationships because of various reasons. As much as I hate divorce personally, I can see the need for a society to allow women to be able to have an out when a man becomes untenable to live with.

Moses, and then the succeeding leaders of Israel who taught on people's rights, tried desperately to give to their people boundaries of truth which introduced proper, ethical ways to live. Without the idea of divorce, then the man would have all authority and never any restraints on doing what he saw fit, which is usually destructive.

The Torah principles which we are just now beginning to be understood fully have been around 5,000 years. Women's rights, children's rights, senior's rights, poor people's rights, animal rights, land conservation, are all clearly spoken of within the Torah as normal society values. There is no other document which makes a balanced society like the Torah. To misunderstand the Torah teachers is to misunderstand the Torah, which they were trying to uphold.

Hillel believed that if anyone saves anyone in this life, then they save the world, if they destroy anyone then they destroy the world. Christian teachers need to do their homework before saying things that are not completely true. We uphold unbalanced people like Martin Luther or the Popes as great teachers of the people, but they usually had a wrong motive behind their teachings. Then we tear down men like Hillel who had good motives.

The reformed wing of today's church has true hearted men, but they use the wrong sources like the Septuagint, thus coming to wrong conclusions about doctrine. If you take a translation such as the Septuagint, and from it extrapolate what the truths should be, you will not be true to the original meaning. It is like shooting an arrow and starting just 1/4 of an inch off; the trajectory of the arrow after 100 yards will have not only missed the bull's-eye but have been completely off the target.

What I see with the churches acceptance of the Greek language, which led to us accepting Greek logic to interpret these Scriptures, we have missed the bull's-eye of truth. In the next chapter we will look briefly at why the original writings of the New Testament are important to find.

# Chapter 8

## Is Scripture Hebrew or Greek?

We need to ask, do we have the Autographs of the New Testament (an autograph is the original document the Apostle or Teacher would have written) and are they important to have? The answer is no, we do not have the autographs. The Christian Scholars of every denomination will set this aside and insist that Greek was the language Paul used. They will teach you that in Paul's letters he uses quotes directly from the Septuagint, which means he taught from this translation.

We have to ask could it have been the people copying and sending Paul's letters out who used the Septuagint quotes instead of the original language, much like we do when we use a theology book not in our own language and then convert it into our own language. We wouldn't keep the original language of the writer in the copy, but instead put in the translation which corresponds to the translation we are reading.

As an example of this, if we were quoting from a German Theologian, we would not use the German language, or the German scripture verse he was using, we would use the best English version we could find and translate it into English. This could very well be the reason the letters we have in Greek used quotes from the Septuagint, to keep the whole text in Greek rather than part Hebrew, which most Greeks would not know. It also could explain why the versions we have are slightly corrupted, and seem to lean more to a Greek audience when they should be more Judaic in thought and feel. When the new language does not have the idioms of the other language the translators usually simplify the words in order for the best possible meanings to get through, this could be the case with many of the Gospels hard to understand conundrums.

Our Bible translations come from these Codices; Sinaiticus, Vaticanus, and Alexandrinus. These copies were all done in the 4$^{th}$ or 5$^{th}$ Century, again these are all guesses, good guesses, but guesses none the less. I am not a proponent of calling into question the texts themselves. I sincerely believe within our Bibles, whether it is Greek, English, French, German, or whatever other language we speak, God's Word is still there.

What I am trying to explain however is, it is not the autographs which means we need to see why we do not have the autographs, and why the scholars just assume Greek is the language God used for the New Testament but not the Old Testament. There is way too much at stake to say the oldest manuscripts we have of the Apostles are in the language they would have used. The Septuagint is not recognized by anyone outside of Christianity as God's real Written Word, this should make us ask why. By real I only mean original.

I am not saying that the Septuagint was not recognized by 1$^{st}$ Century Israeli Scholars as a competent translation, it just was not recognized as the pre-eminent Word of God, this was and still is reserved for Hebrew amongst the Jews. What is amazing to me is how easily the Church took this Greek translation into its heart, believing it is God's pre-eminent Word rather than the Hebrew.

Looking at the Apostles writings through a copy almost 150 years past the date they would have written it; we can still see quite clearly that these men followed a Judaic way of life. Peter alone should alert us to the fact that Jesus clearly taught his Disciples as the other teachers of the day. John and his brother James, and the other Disciples all went from being regular Joes into men who not only followed the truth but emulated it, this could only come through some amazing preparation by their teacher.

Jesus was a Sage of the First Century; his writings have introduced people to a world that few of those days ever experienced, and a world we just take for granted. What I mean is that he taught the same way as the leading teachers of his day, only he taught the masses what the scriptures actually meant not just what they say, this was unheard of. He was questioned by the Pharisees because he was such a powerful Teacher, they wanted to make sure he was using proper Torah principles; he was a threat to the Sadducees and Herodians because He could have led a rebellion against the Emperor very easily, but chose not to.

The ones who really put the kibosh on him were the Herodians and the Sadducees, who were the wealthy that would have lost their position if Rome was thrown out of Israel because the Messiah had come. We always hear it was the Pharisees who decided to kill Jesus, this was not entirely the case, the Sadducees and Herodians were the ones who bribed Judas. In our translations it does say the Pharisees as the main group, but how can this be the case?

When we look at the historical evidence of who the Pharisees were, and who they were not, we see they were not the vindictive group they have been made out to be by our Greek minded forebears, but were regular people who wanted to be conservative Torah Observant people.

They were strict on Torah Observance and quite irritating when they would debate with people who didn't believe like them, but to say they were killers is to misrepresent them. The Orthodox Jews of today are directly linked to the Pharisaical Academies of the 1st Century. Most would be hard-pressed to say these men of today are, or have ever been violent. During the holocaust the men and women from Orthodox Judaism showed their hearts.

There could have been a faction of the Pharisees who were elevating someone else to be the Messiah, which would have given rise to competition. This could mean they would have had to have illicit bedfellows to remove the competition, but to say that the regular Pharisees were the ones who plotted Jesus' death I believe is stretching the truth of who they were as a group.

My hope is that the truth of which actual Pharisees plotted against Jesus will become known. I also hope that we will soon find the real Autographs and see if they are written in Hebrew or Greek.

In the next chapter I will discuss the Hebrew Bible, and the Greek Translation called the Septuagint, and why it is important for the Church to recognize we need to study the Hebrew first then Greek second.

# Chapter 9

# Where are the Original Copies?

The argument over whether the Septuagint, a Greek Translation of the Hebrew Old Testament, also called LXX or Seventy because of how it was made. There were 71 Jewish scholars charged with translating the Hebrew into Greek, why it is called 70 is anyone's guess. As the story goes, all of the Jewish Scholars came up with the exact same version. What was odd was each scholar was in separate rooms and had no contact with one another, there was no comparing and they all made the exact same translation.

Some scholars go on and on about how the Hebrew version that the Jewish people use now is nowhere close to the Septuagint, because the Septuagint was translated from an older unknown Hebrew version of the Scriptures, or they say that the early Christians and Apostles, usually citing Paul, were men who accepted the Greek version as Gods word, so it should be good enough for us. This would seem to be a good conclusion except for the fact that there are too many why questions.

Why would the Apostles, who grew up largely in a Hebrew or Aramaic speaking province turn toward a Hellenistic view of the world? Why would Jesus, who was the Messiah of Israel first, and of the World second, allow his Body, commonly called the church, to turn away from its roots? Why would Paul, a Jewish man who grew up studying all things Judaic, suddenly convert to all things Hellenistic? I think these questions have to have answers.

First we have to understand the Greek translation called the Septuagint and why it became accepted within the church. This is the last piece of why the church went from their Judaic roots, into the Greek way of thinking. Many different scholars have thought and wrote about these things, but because the church has an amazing amount of power, and a reluctance to change, the real truth has never been able to be discussed and then incorporated into life by non-scholars or as we are termed laymen.

I do agree that in some ways this structure has safeguarded the church, but it also introduced an elitism that I do not believe needed to be there. The Roman structure introduced too much corruption and undue influence of the authorities of the day into the church, and created a hierarchy which made the leaders become accustomed to power. This power led to a history of Crusades, the Inquisition, and taking over of Nations like Mexico, Brazil, Latin America, the Philippines, and Puerto Rico by force.

The Church always tries to say the violence which happened in history is not real Christianity and was never sanctioned by the church, but these things were always done by it. Even now, most (not all) Mission organizations are built upon the concept of conquering other cultures with their own brand of culture.

Here is how one Protestant Church sets their mission goals;

*"Develop and maintain a systematic strategy for gospel proclamation and planting churches that will result in the rapid reproduction and multiplication of local indigenous congregations that will make the gospel accessible to all persons among every ethno-linguistic people group;"*

I am not trying to pick on people, I only want to show how missions use conquer and divide programs for their motivations. We see this is a systematic strategy, which means the Missionary goes about to breakdown the weakness of the culture they are ministering in, and then proclaims their brand of Christianity. We also see that the focus is to plant churches, which in reality means making mini mother churches that usually come from the dominant culture of wherever the Missionary is from.

This Mission statement is linear in approach as it seeks to learn how to duplicate successful congregations; this means that if something works, it will be used no matter if it is right or wrong, just as long as it produces results. We also see within this an idea which is only implicit, that is that each of these people's culture and ideas are wrong and they need to come into the same type of lifestyle as the Missionary.

You will probably ask me why this is wrong, isn't this what the Apostle Paul did? Didn't the other Apostles go to preach their brand of world view and set up the Kingdom of the Church? This is where the Greek mentality has given us a completely wrong opinion on how the Gospel is proclaimed, and was proclaimed in the 1st Century.

Gospel proclamation was never a means to an end, it was the end. The Apostles preached the Gospel, Discipled the leaders, and left to proclaim the gospel again. They didn't teach the people how to live; they taught the people who the Messiah was. This is totally different than what is being done today, and what has been done for the last 1,500 years.

Most people I have spoken with say my opinion is wrong, divisive, and short-sighted, they tell me because the Apostles were just beginning and didn't have the man-power or history of being leaders to set up churches like we do now, we couldn't expect them to be as advanced in church planting as we are. I have thought of this for a long time and researched how the Missions community of the last Century has excelled in cross-cultural ministry. I was almost convinced that I was being too hard on the church until I realized one thing. What is the Great Commission all about? Is it a mandate to introduce a new world-view and culture, as is being done across the Nations today, or are we just called to proclaim the Gospel, teach the people the principles of belief, and then move on?

In the Greek language, the Great Commission is about authority to command obedience, and then command that obedience of others in Jesus' Name. In Hebrew however the Great Commission means proclaiming to people to be Disciples of the Lord, and then allow them to obey Jesus, not force them. I will give you two quotes, one translated from the Greek into English and the other one translated from the Hebrew in to English.

*Matthew 28:19-20 "Therefore go and make disciples of all nations, baptizing them in the name of the Father and of the Son and of the Holy Spirit, and teaching them to obey everything I have commanded you. And surely I am with you always, to the very end of the age." NIV*

*Matthew 28:19-20 "Therefore, go and make people from all nations into talmidim, immersing them into the reality of the Father, the Son and the Ruach HaKodesh, and teaching them to obey everything that I have commanded you. And remember! I will be with you always, yes, even until the end of the age." Complete Jewish Bible*

The differences are very subtle and most people would say they are only semantics, but look at the differences with me for a moment. Both verses essentially say the same thing, Go and Make Disciples right. How the Disciples are made however is different with only one phrase changed, instead of saying baptize in, which is a finished action once completed (linear in thought), it says immerse in the reality of, this is subtle but much different. To immerse someone in the reality of something, means that it will take time to allow these people learn the lessons needed to be Disciples; the Greek version sounds more like lining up at the buffet line and making a plate of food. First you get the salad, then the soup, then the main course and vegetable, and finish it off with some dessert. One is neat and tidy; the other is a lifelong process.

I have to explain why I believe the Septuagint, while being a good translation, should not be the main base of our English translations. When you have a third hand translation as you do when you translate the Old Testament from the Greek into English or other secondary language. You miss almost all of the idioms and nuances of the original language because it is a second generation translation. I challenge you to read an Old Testament version that was translated from the Hebrew rather than the Greek (David Sterns *"The Complete Jewish Bible"* is a beautiful Translation of English from Hebrew). You will find that the word pictures are clearer, and it is a much more positive thought provoking translation overall. I am not talking about reading this for one or two times. I mean read only this type of translation for a year or so to get used to the beauty of it, then go back to an NIV or NASB and see the difference.

I do not know how honest people who know how to read Greek and Hebrew cannot see the simple fact that any Greek language Scripture is a translation of the true Scripture. I am really simple in this but will try to show how silly it is to say the Septuagint is better than the Hebrew Scriptures.

Anytime you have a copy, no matter how nice it is, can never compare to the original. First we will look at why Hebrew is the original language of the Scriptures. Hebrew is known to have come into being around the same time as Moses brought down the Scriptures from Mt Sinai. Moses brought the Torah to the Israelites around 5,000 years ago, some scholars say that Hebrew originated much later but I believe that it was only used much later, it originated with Moses at Mt Sinai. Of course, to prove this assumption is very difficult, and will only happen when we find the original Ten Commandments written by the finger of God.

Hebrew is also the only language on the planet where the letters actually speak of the One True God and Judaic principles, scholars again say that Hebrew was made to say these things. For this objection I think we have to use the path of faith, we need to ask does the language define the society, or does the society make the language, this is the conundrum we are facing here. The age-old, *"what came first the chicken or the egg",* question is proper here. I believe in this case the chicken (Hebrew) came first.

To understand the Hebrew Alphabet you need to realize why Hebrew came into being. The Etymology of languages are a difficult science, but because there has been so much made about Hebrew there is a mountain of information on this particular language. Non-Jewish scholars say that Hebrew is part of the Northern Semitic languages, specifically a proto-Canaanite dialect. The Hebrew Language, according to these scholars was spoken around the $10^{th}$ Century BCE (Before Common Era), and had its most use in the $6^{th}$ Century BCE, during the time of the Babylonian exile of Israel.

In *Genesis 10:21it says*

*"Sons were also born to Shem, whose older brother was Japheth; Shem was the ancestor of all the sons of Eber."*

Ibri or the plural form Ibrim is one name for the Israelite people; this is derived from the name Eber, Ibri means to "cross-over". Eber was reportedly Abraham's ancestor so any language from Abraham is Semitic because of this tie, and Hebrew is derived from the name Eber, so Hebrew is a Semitic language.

There is a lot of evidence that Hebrew was used within Israel. Some of the verses which prove that Israel used this language as an everyday language come from 2 Kings 18:27, and Isa. 36:11. There are also coins, letters, and other documents found at Archaeological sites which prove that it was a spoken language for quite a long time. The Nation of Israel has revived it again so it is guaranteed to have a new resurgence in understanding.

Why is the etymology of the Hebrew language important to look at? If we understand where it comes from we can better make the choice on which language we need to follow in respect to our Scriptures. I think Hebrew has a very clear record of being about, and handed down as, God's Word.

If we study the letters themselves they all speak about different aspects of Torah principles. Hebrew also personalizes God in ways that other languages do not. The personal Name of the Creator for example is only in Hebrew. This collection of vowels YHVH, can only mean Gods Name, no other language has this Word.

In English if we say God, it could the Supreme Deity, or just a certain person's, or groups deity, it is a general term. The Hebrew word for God is the personal name for God; I do not think you can get any easier than that to understand which language we should use.

Within Greek there are personal names for Zeus or other Pagan Deities, but not one for the One True God, it is a general term used. There are secular and Christian scholars who try to say that the root meanings of Hebrew terms come from pagan belief like Greek, but the people whose ancestors spoke the language say this is not the case, for my money I trust the person who speaks the language over the ones who are just trying to study it with a pre-conceived notion.

Some secular, or Christian scholars have even tried to say that Hebrew is not any more special than Greek, and seem to intimate that Hebrew is actually a lower language than Greek. There are also many supposed scholars who try to emphatically teach that Greek was the only language that the Apostles used. They also use an argument that says, because of the differences in the Hebrew within the Bible Books themselves that the Greek translation is better than using Hebrew.

I would say to these people, we are still talking about Hebrew in the books, not another language. There is a bit of a difference in conjugation, or a difference in a word construction, but this takes nothing away from the context or meaning of the passages in question. Whoever says that a translation is better than the original seems to me wants to prove another theory rather than follow the truth.

The Talmud teaches a theory about why Israel speaks Hebrew. This theory teaches that because only Israel out of all the 70 Nations of that era said yes to Gods question of will you follow and obey they received the divine language. I think it is interesting to consider that this teaching is true; in my heart I believe it to be true. Whether it is or isn't does not matter, what matters is that the God we serve came from a Hebrew centered World, not a Greek speaking one.

Let's look at the Greek Language and see if maybe God wants to use it to reveal His Word to the World. The Greek language belongs to the Indo-European family of languages. It has been around for about the same amount of time as Hebrew has been spoken, give or take a couple hundred years. Greek derives its alphabet from the Phoenician script, as does Hebrew. Greeks did modify their alphabet in order to make their vowel sounds into script, whereas Classical or Biblical Hebrew never had these vowel scripts, and only until recently has had them. This is important because without vowels it is difficult to understand what the words mean unless you're a master of the language.

I believe Greek became so widespread because of their vowel creation. Greek has definitely been a blessing to the World. Without it, the world would be much different; it is one of the first to be considered as a multicultural language, or one that was like Aramaic, as it was used by more than one country as a main language.

The Rabbi's teach that the Greek language had a dispensation of God's blessings in order to be used as a translation for God's

Word, some people wouldn't consider this as important but I do because it shows that translations are an important part of how God reveals His message to the World. The Rabbi's also teach that this translation was confined to Greek speaking people in this dispensation as Gods Word.

The main problem I have with Greek as a language the Apostles would have chosen to use to make their truths known is the fact that they knew they were speaking the Words of God, and knew also they were confirming the Words of the Son of God. The Greek terminology would have been foreign to their minds and ears in respect to portraying the concepts and meanings they were trying to portray. The church has minimized this by just accepting that the Apostles would have used Koine Greek. Koine Greek was the main language of Rome and Roman Cities, Jerusalem was never a Roman City, nor would have they been comfortable with this language.

There are many Jewish Historians who say that Greek was common in Israel; but only for the High Priests, the Sadducees, and the merchants who wanted to trade in the

Roman Cities. This would explain why the Sadducees and High Priest Caiaphas knew Greek, but Jesus and his followers probably would not have known Greek, because none of them were part of the Government except one who was a tax collector, and we do not know of any that were merchants.

My belief that the Autographs were Hebrew does have some legs, as the Gospel of Matthew which was written by Matthew (the tax collector), would have known Greek because he was a government official, has been found in a Hebrew version, which is ironic because if any of the Gospels would have been in Greek it would have been his writing.

I am not saying that we need to be Jewish to understand the Scriptures, nor do we need to give up everything we know, but we need to rethink what we use to understand Gods Word. We have an opportunity to re-engage this topic of interpretation and source discussion because of the explosion of knowledge.

Barring the Lords Return, which I hope is soon, we need as a church to become more honest and forthright in speaking up rather than leaving these types of discussions to the supposed experts. I talk to many people about these things and most of the reactions I get are people think it's not very important to know about whether we use Hebrew or Greek as a source.

How can this not be important? We have allowed a pagan culture and worldview to show us what our Scriptures mean. To me this is untenable. We have allowed a culture which put mystery religions over doing what was right. We have also allowed a culture that used a pagan system of logic to show us how to interpret our Scriptures.

We allowed a pagan ruler to organize our churches or to at least help us to organize ourselves. We now use the Greek leadership system, and follow its philosophical truth which has now been dead for a long time.

Instead of allowing the Lord to lead and direct us we embraced this belief of domination. Rather than be examples of truth, we learned to be clubs for truth. Not because of the truth, please do not misunderstand me, but because of the system we became caught into. Let's change this, let's stand up and say we have had enough of allowing others to write the future for us, let's follow the Holy Spirit and do as He wants.

# Chapter 10

## Should we look like a Greek or Hebrew?

Hebrew was the language God chose to reveal Himself in, to say the Septuagint is equal to the Hebrew version is to forget about 2,000 years of prior Biblical knowledge and Revelation. The church of the 4th and 5th Century however, did just this, and we are left with a Greek thinking, Greek looking, and most absurd to me, Greek sounding Scriptures. This is not just for Scholars to debate over, I believe that all of us Believers need to look at the evidence of what we believe and why, and change now so our children can go down a clearer path than we have.

Here is a quote from one of Origen's teachings on why the Leaders of his day should be considered as High Priests in the Order of Melchizedek;

*"But those who devote themselves to the divine word and have no other employment but the service of God may not unnaturally, allowing for the difference of occupation in the two cases, be called our Levites and priests. And those who fulfil a more distinguished*

*office than their kinsmen will perhaps be high-priests, according to the order of Aaron, not that of Melchisedek. Here someone may object that it is somewhat too bold to apply the name of high-priests to men, when Jesus Himself is spoken of in many a prophetic passage as the one great priest, as "We have a great high-priest who has passed through the heavens, Jesus, the Son of God." But to this we reply that the Apostle clearly defined his meaning, and declared the prophet to have said about the Christ, "Thou art a priest forever, according to the order of Melchisedek," and not according to the order of Aaron. We say accordingly that men can be high-priests according to the order of Aaron, but according to the order of Melchisedek only the Christ of God."*

Now let's look at a quote below to get a sense of how the First Century Bishop Ignatius (a Greek Intellectual), taught and viewed Scripture, it is radically different than Origen,

*"It is good to teach, if he who speaks also acts. For he who shall both "do and teach, the same shall be great in the kingdom."*(The Shema is recited everyday by Torah

---

Observant people and this is the main teaching of it, Duet. 6:4-9)

*Our Lord and God, Jesus Christ, the Son of the living God, first did and then taught, as Luke testifies, "whose praise is in the Gospel through all the Churches." There is nothing which is hid from the Lord, but our very secrets are near to Him. Let us therefore do all things as those who have Him dwelling in us, which we may be His temples, and He may be in us as God. Let Christ speak in us, even as He did in Paul.* (The Temple seemed to still be a crutch for the people of this day. The Torah speaks much about Temple Sacrifice, and it had just ended when these teachings were written. We do not even think of a physical Temple where real sacrifices for sins happened, these people saw the Aaronic Priests fulfilling Torah Commands about sacrifice, this was the part of Torah buried with Christ. In the Temple was where the people heard Gods voice, felt safe because of the High Priest who heard from God for everyone, it was where they celebrated the Holidays, and remembered what God told them to do, it was a physical manifestation of the heavenly realm where God was, now these people were being taught this all happens in the heart, it was difficult.)

*Let the Holy Spirit teach us to speak the things of Christ in like manner as He did." And again "Stand fast, brethren, in the faith of Jesus Christ, and in His love, in His passion, and in His resurrection. Do ye all come together in common, and individually, through grace, in one faith of God the Father, and of Jesus Christ His only-begotten Son, and "the first-born of every creature," but of the seed of David according to the flesh, being under the guidance of the Comforter, in obedience to the bishop and the presbytery with an undivided mind, breaking one and the same bread, which is the medicine of immortality, and the antidote which prevents us from dying, but a cleansing remedy driving away evil* (sounds more like the Evil Urge to sin rather than a prison of the flesh), *[which causes] that we should live in God through Jesus Christ."*

Let's read a second Century Leader, the Pastor of Hermas;

*"First of all, believe that there is one God who created and finished all things, and made all things out of nothing. He alone is able to contain the whole, but Himself*

*cannot be contained.* (The Jews call God the *Great Cause* this sounds almost identical to this concept, not an unconnected Deity which came from the Greek pantheon belief system) *Have faith therefore in Him, and fear Him; and fearing Him, exercise self-control. Keep these commands, and you will cast away from you all wickedness, and put on the strength of righteousness, and live to God, if you keep this commandment.* (Sounds like the Evil Urge to sin being taught about)

*"Fear," said he, "the Lord, and keep His commandments. For if you keep the commandments of God, you will be powerful in every action, and every one of your actions will be incomparable.* (Here there are two types of commandments, God or Torah Commands, and Jesus' commands of obedience, both are needed)

*For, fearing the Lord, you will do all things well. This is the fear which you ought to have, that you may be saved.*

*But fear not the devil; for, fearing the Lord, you will have dominion over the devil, for there is no power in him. But he in whom there is no power ought on no account to be an object of fear; but He in whom there is glorious power is truly to be feared.*

Here are some teachings by 2nd Century Theophilus of Antioch (not the one in Acts)

*"You will say, then, to me: "You said that God ought not to be contained in a place, and how do you now say that He walked in Paradise?" Hear what I say. The God and Father, indeed, of all cannot be contained, and is not found in a place, for there is no place of His rest; but His Word, through whom He made all things, being His power and His wisdom, assuming the person of the Father and Lord of all, went to the garden in the person of God, and conversed with Adam* (Sounds like the Living Torah and the Great Cause).

*For the divine writing itself teaches us that Adam said that he had heard the voice.*(Sounds like the Torah which are known now as the teachings of righteousness to the Torah Observant Jews)

*But what else is this voice but the Word of God, who is also His Son? Not as the poets and writers of myths talk of the sons of gods begotten from intercourse [with women], but as truth expounds, the Word, that always exists, residing within the heart of God. For before anything came into being*

He had Him as a counsellor, being His own mind and thought (sounds to me like he is refuting the Greek philosophy we are now following).

Let's now read a 3<sup>rd</sup> Century Leader Tertullian discussing truth

*"Being, therefore, observers of "seasons" for these things, and of "days, and months, and years," we Galaticize. Plainly we do, if we are observers of Jewish ceremonies, of legal solemnities: for those the apostle unteaches, suppressing the continuance of the Old Testament which has been buried in Christ* (Could this merely be Temple Sacrifices and Levitical Tithing which in this day was a big part of a Jews life), *and establishing that of the New* (could the new merely mean celebrating Belief in Jesus' sacrifice, rather than actual sacrifices and realizing that the Temple Sacrifices were truly over, as well as the Temple itself).

*But if there is a new creation in Christ, our solemnities too will be bound to be new: else, if the apostle has erased all devotion absolutely "of seasons, and days, and months, and years," why do we celebrate the Passover by an annual rotation in the first month?* (It seems that the Torah Holidays were pretty important still)

*Why in the fifty ensuing days do we spend our time in all exultation? Why do we devote to Stations the fourth and sixth days of the week, and to fasts the "preparation-day?"* (Here we get a glimpse that the 3rd Century Church Celebrated Biblical Holidays, but not Pharisaical fence laws about those Holidays; it sounds like this teaching is refuting an argument about someone not wanting to follow Torah Principles)

These are very interesting quotes, quotes which are much different in content than our present day teachers teach. You expect the writings to be a little different since they are almost 2000 years old, but if you compare them to Origen's teachings you still see a major difference. These men are teaching like the Apostle Paul did in Romans and 1 & 2 Corinthians, whereas Origen taught like Socrates or Plato, or the Philosophers of the day. The differences to me are staggering.

After the 3rd Century, the Fathers of the Church began to use much more pronounced Greek logic in their writings; we see a big shift in how the Church studies within this timeframe became Greek, and an even bigger shift in how much honor is accorded its leaders. Most of the writings before the Third Century, when the people were told to give honor to the leaders, it was to encourage the people to listen to the truth, not to put the leaders on a pedestal. After the Third Century it seemed there was a shift in language which said obedience to the leaders were just as important as emulating the teaching they brought.

I want to ask why the Church went this way? Why would the Church Leaders choose a philosophical mindset that Jesus never had, and embrace it so totally that they end up completely ruining their relationship with their Jewish brothers?

The 2$^{nd}$ Century Church was radically different than the church of the 3$^{rd}$ and 4$^{th}$ Century. The Council of Nicaea changed the church in a big way because the church went from being persecuted to almost overnight being the State Religion and the persecutor. I realize the Church could never have absorbed this without some radical upgrading of their systems, I just wish they wouldn't have used the Plato and Socrates system to upgrade the Church.

21 years before the Council of Nicaea in 325, there was one of the worst persecutions of all time by Emperor Diocletian in the

year of 303 AD, he tried to wipe out the Christians completely in the Eastern part of the Empire. They burned writings, scrolls, books, and anything else that spoke of Jesus or the Apostles. There were whole villages of Christians burned to death and much suffering of believers in this time.

The persecution that happened during this time was wrote about the most because in just 306 AD, three years after the persecution, Constantine became Emperor and restored Christians to legal status, as well as gave back lands and other things stolen from them, so this persecution was one of the ones able to be recounted of in writings and stories which have survived for the most part.

It is interesting to note that with no more persecutions per se, of the Christians, there was no more burning of materials, and because by this time the Judaic part of the Church had become small, due to Israel and the Jews suffering their own persecution under the Romans, it was now the Greek minded believers who flooded the churches with their own books and leanings. It's also interesting to note that the Oldest Codices come from this time frame of the Church; there are no earlier documents of the Apostles.

I find this history to almost conclusively prove that if nothing else, we cannot know what the Autograph copies of the Apostles Letters and Gospels were in respect to language, because copies we have were from this tumultuous period and were sent out to a predominantly Greek Speaking Church. Who would have had the actual autographs, my guess would be men like Polycarp (who was the last living Disciple of the Apostle John), who died by being burned on a stake, after his scrolls were burned. To find any autographs will be a true miracle, one I am praying for.

Even the leaders of the Church in Jerusalem during the 3$^{rd}$ and 4$^{th}$ Century were Gentiles, so the line of Judaic minded leaders in Israel had ended with Judas of Jerusalem (or Judah Kyriako's), who was said to be the great grandson of Jude, Jesus' brother. Judas was replaced by a gentile named Mark in AD 136, who was appointed by the Bishop of Caesarea according to the Catholic tradition (again suspect because of their wanting to lay the foundation of Greek thinking and Peter as the head of the Church);

this appointment came after the Bar Kokhba rebellion that finally removed all the Jews from Israel.

After the persecution of 306AD The Church as a whole was in disarray for sure. The people went through one of the worst trials they ever had. Their materials were burned; leaders and their families killed, villages wiped out and pagans moved into their homes, and other villages turned back to paganism to avoid the persecution. Within this malaise of emotions of confusion, fear, and hopelessness, Constantine was seen as a liberator.

The first Council conducted in 325 at Nicaea by Constantine I, was the very first time that Christians became powerful and elevated in the Roman Empire. The Historian Eusebius played a big part in this celebration of Christianity because he is spoken of extensively as the mediator between the two factions of Christians, one believing the Arian Doctrine and the other wanting an anti-Arian Doctrine, the anti-Arian Doctrine won from Palestine which opened the Church to Origen's teachings.

Eusebius was a proponent of Origen's writings. He was close friends with a Disciple of Origen named Pamphilius who started a school to teach Origen's doctrines in Palestine.

When we look at the influence Origen had on the Church we see it was positive in the beginning because it allowed for the continuation of the Church, there would be no telling what could have happened if Constantine would have chosen Mithraism as the main Religion of the Empire.

When Origen moved the dialogue away from Judaic idioms, phrases, and Hebrew word understandings into a realm of common Greek idioms and the logic of the day by using only Greek language and logic, this made the Church much easier to be understood by the masses.

The Pagan religion followers were in a vacuum after having their religions stripped of authority in front of their eyes and needed to have this vacuum filled with what was comfortable, I believe this is why from the time of Constantine to now, the Church has always officially stated that it was the true Worship of God and replaced Israel. This may seem simplistic and not very orthodox, but look into the history, and compare these things and see what your conclusion is.

As the Church left its Judaic Roots and embraced the Greek philosophical approach, the Jews became problems for the Christians because of their insistence on a Judaic Worldview, understood through their rabbinic authorities. There was a tendency to view the Jews as Christ killers, and persecute them first if anything bad happened in the Empire. This prejudice carried over after the Romans were long gone, and has only recently stopped because of the Holocaust where 6 million Jews were killed just because they were Jewish.

Officially the Catholic Church, Eastern Orthodox, and most other Christian Churches in North America believe that the New Covenant fulfilled and replaced the Mosaic or Old Covenant. These groups of believers also believe that the reason the Jews are still around is because the gifts of God are irrevocable, this phrase is from the Catholic version on Supercessionism or Replacement Theology, but it sums up what most Christians believe about the Jews. After the

Holocaust these proclamations have begun to almost never be heard, but officially the Church stands by its doctrines adopted in the $3^{rd}$ - $5^{th}$ Century of its existence.

In today's day and age the church has tried very hard to remove this stigma, but from the $3^{rd}$ Century we can see the foundations of why Church people consider themselves better than others runs deep and is almost not able to be changed unless they get rid of Greek logic and realize they are the grafted in ones, not the Israeli's.

*2 Timothy 2:15 "Do your best to present yourself to God as one approved, a worker who does not need to be ashamed and who correctly handles the word of truth."*

Paul stated this as some of his last encouragements to his son in the Faith Timothy. These two books have always been important to me. If we read these books we see a true Disciple of the Lord does not just accept what has always been, but studies to make sure he/she believes what has been taught and why it has been taught. I will say it again; we need to start making decisions about the future of how we study.

If we stay the course of Greek thinking, in the next 50 years the Church will not even believe in the resurrection properly. We will have the teaching but it will be twisted into something that will fit into the pop culture of the day. In the next chapter I will try to give more practical ways of why we need to study in a Judaic way rather than a Greek way.

# Chapter 11

## Early Church Fathers Teachings

The first Early Church Writings I loved was from a man named Polycarp, who was Discipled by John the Apostle. This man was well into old age before being martyred by the Romans, sometime in the first Century around159 A.D. He had a very simple faith, but one underscored by Rabbinic Wisdom he learned from his own teacher, the Apostle John who I spoke about earlier in the book. Here is a taste of Polycarp's teachings;

*Wherefore, girding up your loins," "serve the Lord in fear, and truth, as those who have forsaken the vain, empty talk and error of the multitude, and "believed in Him who raised up our Lord Jesus Christ from the dead, and gave Him glory," and a throne at His right hand. To Him all things" in heaven and on earth are subject. Him every spirit serves.*

*He comes as the Judge of the living and the dead. His blood will God require of those who do not believe in Him.*

*But He who raised Him up from the dead will raise up us also, if we do His will, and walk in His commandments, and love what He loved, keeping ourselves from all unrighteousness, covetousness, love of money, evil speaking, false witness; "not rendering evil for evil, or railing for railing," or blow for blow, or cursing for cursing, but being mindful of what the Lord said in His teaching:*

*"Judge not, that ye be not judged; forgive, and it shall be forgiven unto you; be merciful, that ye may obtain mercy; with what measure ye mete, it shall be measured to you again; and once more, "Blessed are the poor, and those that are persecuted for righteousness' sake, for theirs is the kingdom of God."*

From his Writings and others, I saw a formula for understanding Jesus' teachings. This formula didn't become clear to me however, until I took a class about Exegetical Processes. It was this class, which would send me to research a passage I had never heard of up to that moment. This passage was Dt. 6:4-9, as I spoke of earlier in this book.

I now know this is called the Shema of Israel. It is what has bound the Tribe of Judah together through their wanderings. It is their anchor. When I looked at this verse I needed to use the original language, which is Hebrew. I read amazing truths about the passage; they were from Ancient Rabbinic writing, men who hadn't lived here for literally thousands of years.

What's more, the Rabbis sounded much like Jesus and the Apostles writings I read, as well as the first Century Writers I had read like Polycarp. It was amazing to me how much Godly wisdom and understanding these men had. I was nervous because I had heard the Jews were people who would spit in your face if you mentioned Jesus' name.

I had also heard that the Orthodox Jews believed someone in New York was their Savior. Once I got to know the Orthodox views, I realized this was wrong. I had no idea these were men were just like me, wanting only to do what they felt in their heart to do.

I went from these initial writings to more recent Jewish Writings. To Men like:

❖ Rashi (1000 a.d.)

❖ Rabbi Ovadiah Sforno (1450-1500 a.d.)

❖ The Baal Shem Tov (1698-1760 a.d.)

❖ Rabbi Meir HaKohen Kagan or the Chofetz Chaim
(1800-1900)

❖ Rabbi Abraham J. Twerski (1930-present)

There are many others but these were the ones who
made the most impact on me. Within this spectrum of Jewish
Wisdom writings, I found a basis for daily prayer, daily
Study, why it's important to share our salvation, how to
evangelize, why Biblical Holidays were important. Basically,
the Jewish people knew the reasons we believe and Worship
the One True God.

These men were not trying to teach me, a Christian,
anything at all. These books simply contain the historical
concepts, proper understandings, and Biblical logic handed
down from Moses' day until now.

All these men had historical proof, contextual proof,
and legal proof, of how they could confidently affirm what
they knew. We as Christians confidently affirm what we

think is true at the time, but these truths seem to change if the societal facts tell us that our assumptions are wrong.

When teaching, I usually felt I was confidently affirming something I desired to be true rather than having a concrete basis for this truth. Things like why God hears our prayers, why we need to pray, what Jesus meant in His Gospels about how to love your neighbor as yourself, how to be kind to those who persecute you, how to be a light to the world, and what your light actually is. I could go on, but the Greek way to study these things usually only takes you down a path of Word Studies or proof texts after you come up with a subject you want to teach about.

Both of these methods, Word Studies and Proof Texts, are inadequate when trying to Disciple people who have questions like, why is homosexuality a sin if it is inherent in my DNA. We can state the obvious of course, say it is a sinful lifestyle and needs to be repented of. We can explain why sin came into the world, although it leaves a lot of questions. Then we have to explain why we do not believe in the Law but still use it in respect to homosexuality.

We can also walk the person through other discipleship methods based on definitions of English terms we find in the Bible, but I find that this becomes something which does not stick. Thankfully the Holy Spirit has been with us Gentiles for the past 1500 years so we could find the way out of sin. Without the Holy Spirit we would truly be schizophrenic people, because we say things are wrong on the one hand, but can never back up why it is wrong.

Without Torah Principles we can never say what sin is and what isn't. Without the Torah we cannot explain what righteous life looks like. Without the Torah we cannot explain why humankind needs Jesus. Without the Torah it's difficult to understand what Jesus taught in the Gospels.

I find Torah Principles rooted and grounded in clear and precise biblical philosophy, much better than just telling someone to believe and everything will be ok. Torah principles are not about being righteous. Only in Jesus' death and resurrection do we become righteous, but after we become believers we need to grow and mature. To do this we need to lay firm foundations in our lives, not hopes and dreams from a Greek language rooted in paganism.

When teaching Jesus' sayings you either have to have amazing stories to wow people, or give them Greek word studies which bore people to tears. You can load up on cross reference Scriptures which may or may not fit into the context of what you're teaching about, but they make your points. Either way, because of the shallow aspect of these methods of teaching, most messages are forgotten about ten minutes after the person leaves the Church.

It's frustrating to honestly try and have a deep connection with the Lord but have it reduced to needing to go back to the first time you believe to feel like your connected. As a church person most of us feel like we only grow in the knowledge of the church doctrines, not closer in prayer, closer in devotion, and closer in knowing the Lord. We feel powerful emotions for sure, but the principles we need to translate those emotions to actions are contained in a part of the Scriptures we say has been finished and have no relevance now.

Jesus taught from long held Torah principles. He was teaching the deepest level of interpretation, giving what the Jews call Halacha, this means legal precedents on how to walk out Torah principles. Jesus taught to do, not think. His audience knew the references he was making, we as Gentiles, using a watered down Greek translation miss much of the truth He was trying to give us.

The Jewish Orthodox Rabbis of today teach the basis that Jesus had. I found believers and Orthodox Jews are on the same team, Worshiping the same God, trying to walk in the same character traits, only we as Gentiles needed the Messiah and focused on Him solely, and the Jews focused on the Sinai experience, the giving of the Torah.

Both of us trusting in the Living Word of God, just one an older version and one a newer. I hope to not offend with this language but this is how I see it. The Living Torah whether written, or embodied in the person of Jesus is the most important to follow in my opinion.

Both of these Religions, Judaism and Christianity, had the exact same rules, only one refused to realize it. The Church was the one missing the playing field, because instead of realizing that Jesus didn't come here to take anything away. He came here to fulfill and teach how to do what was already in place in Israel, we as the Church miss half of what Jesus brought to us, because we are so caught up in the Greek way of life.

The Rabbis are not like the people of Islam, or other Cults, who do not follow the true Scriptures, and make things up when they get confused. These men have the same goals as us, the same morals, the same concepts, but a much deeper understanding of why. When I first saw these things I was amazed because I knew that these were people with the answers I was searching for. I hoped my other Christian friends would also be excited to learn these truths.

What I found was anything but excitement, it was major resistance.

I heard phrases like "Do these men believe in Jesus?" or

"Are they Christians?" said with contempt in my friend's voice

I also heard accusatory questions like,

"So, you think doing the Law makes you better than me?" And my favorite was.

"If you do the Law then you have left Grace, Brother!"

I trusted the people who spoke these questions, so I looked into their questions deeply. I asked the question. Do these Rabbis believe in the Messiah of Israel? I saw that the Jews as we know them are really only the Tribe of Judah, and according to their 13 principles of faith did believe in Israel's Messiah. Only their Messiah was the Jesus of the First Century, not the 20$^{th}$ Century Greek looking Messiah the Church peddles today.

The Church uses terms like, "the Jews refused the New Covenant", or "they rejected Jesus therefore are rejected", or "they don't believe in Jesus therefore cannot be saved". Some churches do believe that Israel will be 'saved' in the end, but it has to be as they were saved or they will not be in heaven.

There were people who would dance to what they deemed Messianic or Jewish music, and use Hebrew phrases, but would stop short if I questioned them further about the Jews being Godly, or the Talmud being a good document to study. These people wanted to feel like they were Jewish, as many of their names told them they were, but they still used the linear Greek way of thinking which meant that they could not use the Judaic way of interpretation and missed so much depth and understanding.

What really alerted me to a problem that was brewing in the church, had to be that most of the people who said they followed Jesus with all their heart, could never say Israel was first and gentiles second. It seemed to them that their internal logic told them that Israel had lost their place, and we (Gentiles) had taken their place. Of course these people would say with genuine smiles that when the Jews start proclaiming the Gospel according to reformed Theology, they will be back in control of how God operates on the Planet. Until that time however these people believe we are in control of how God moves and works on the planet.

In all these things, I became very confused and alone. I took the stance however, that people who know what they believe, surely are better than those who only desire their beliefs to be true. When we look at Judaic History of belief and the Churches History of belief there is a startling contrast to the two. The only genuine beliefs the Church has held onto since the First Century has been; the belief that Jesus is Messiah, and that His Apostles teachings are the ones we should follow. Everything else has been turned around so much that no one knows what is real or what is not.

As one example I will use, is the way we as a Church take the apocalyptic teachings, there are four distinct views on how Jesus will come back. There is the Idealist (Allegorical View, Amillennial), the Preterist (Partial Fulfillment of Prophecy, Amillennial), the Historicist (Protestant Reformation View, Postmillennial), and the Futurist ( Pre, Mid or Post-Tribulation). These are four views that have only one commonality to them, Jesus is the Messiah, everything else is different. Within these four views are huge blocks of the church that can never really fellowship with one another because of how they think, not what they do, but how they think. This is an example of why the Greek thinking has to end in the church.

I want to fellowship with my Brethren from each of these views, but as soon as you become good friends what happens is arguments and then division over thinking. This should not factor into who we fellowship with but it does, this to me is so very wrong, but because of our Greek linear world view we fall in this trap all too often.

The Torah Observant Jews however, have really not changed their beliefs very much; they still follow Torah Principles, and try as best they can to stay to what Moses taught them. They do get into heated debates about how, why and where to put on Tefillin, or lay Tefillin as they say, and sometimes it causes them to start different groups, but they think the same way and realize they do.

There will always be different perspectives within groups, with one group being more Orthodox than another, but with the people who believe that the Torah is God's Word given at Mt Sinai to Moses, their belief system and morality has basically stayed the same in the past 2,000 years. Does this make them better or worse than the Christians in my mind, no, it only speaks to how they follow.

This type of continuity and pureness is what the Church needs to have in the coming years. There are so many denominations that have stopped reproducing themselves because they stayed in the culture of when their denomination had started.

The Church has rethought their Orthodoxy over ten times in the past 1500 years, just this last 100 years with all the influx of freedom in how we believe has created a mish-mash of belief's which is chaotic at best, neurotic at worst.

The Church in the 4<sup>th</sup> Century decided to embrace the Greek style of thought, which begins with the core sciences, then goes into Philosophy, and finally ends with you choosing your personal belief. We can see how destructive this formula has been to the churches around North America, and Europe, as they started building Colleges seeking out the core sciences, and now those Colleges have become places where kids lose their Faith rather than deepen it.

You may ask yourself how Judaic Interpretation can explain what the Church should do and bring everyone together, if it was specifically to the Nation of Israel. First we as a Church Body need to realize that Jesus was a Torah Observant Jew, who never said Torah Observance was wrong. What he said about the Pharisees fence laws were that some were wrong and should be done away with, not the basis for those fence laws, but the fence law itself. Jesus wanted to gather Israel so they would realize that they were all on the same team, but they wouldn't and because of this dissension within the Tribes were scattered in what is called the Diaspora.

Please do not misunderstand me, the Diaspora was going to happen whether they believed Jesus as their Messiah or not, what they missed out by not accepting their Messiah was the joy of knowing Jesus the Son of God. I say this because Jesus prophesied in Matthew 28:1-4 that the Temple would be destroyed, and it was, He also taught that He had other Nations (us) to bring into the fold, and He has.

All the things that have happened in the last 2000 years are not a mistake, they were going to happen. The Jews aren't the bad guys here setting things in motion because of unbelief, they were judged long before Jesus came. Believing in the Messiah would not have eliminated them from being scattered, but it would just have allowed them to be one with the Torah they love, as Jesus is the Living Torah. The Tribe of Judah was the last one to be scattered and happened after the Bar Kokhba rebellion.

Most Orthodox Rabbis, regardless of group, teach that the Diaspora happened because the twelve tribes could not get along with each other, and because of this they had to be exiled so when they come back together they will realize Unity is the best thing. They teach that unity does not happen because of good feeling, but it has to have pillars to support it.

These pillars they say are; realization Israel is one in heart and Mind (Isa. 2:4, Jeremiah 30), realization that the Torah directive of Proper Speech has to be obeyed (Isa. 2:4), realization that the Torah is central to their life in Israel (Hosea 3), and a realization that the Messiah is a reality (Isaiah 59:20).

All of Jesus' own teachings are centered on Torah Principles. Jesus said that he was bringing us gentiles, into His Fold (Jn. 10:19). Jesus wanted us to realize the amazing historical faith we are being brought into. The Nation of Israel was already in the Fold.

Are we Israelites? NO, but we are His Children and because of this we are heirs to His promises, which mean we need to Study Torah through Him.

The Church (or the Congregation of Gentiles who follow the Messiah) is basically comprised of a group of

Gentiles, from different Nations, tribes, and tongues, who will never become the Nation of Israel. We, by our very nature cannot be Israel, nor can we hope to enter into Gods truth without Jesus bringing us there.

To understand Jesus and his message of hope, love, and forgiveness, it is incumbent upon us to Study the Torah to see what Jesus meant when he said phrases like ...*Love your neighbor as yourself......be lights.....you are the Salt of the Earth* .... Jesus was a Torah Observant Jew, living within a Torah Observant World.

I believe He desires for us to understand why the Torah is "Teachings of Righteousness" and not "Laws". If we accept who we are, who the Nation of Israel is, and realize the Torah Principles are important to learn from, our walk in an Israeli Messiah will make much more sense and have a deeper meaning in our life, it will not only be a cultural thing to do when we are in trouble, or something our parents taught us. We will all come to the foot of the cross ourselves and realize that we all have a choice to say **we** will do and obey, or we will not. It starts with us opening up our hearts and embracing a Judaic mindset that Jesus and His Apostles had.

# Chapter 12

## What is Torah Study?

I believe the Tribe of Judah has kept the Words of God, as is their purpose, and we as Believers in their Messiah, should understand what the basis of our Messiah's teachings are. This understanding is only found in the Torah.

By Torah I mean the Teachings of Righteousness. The Law has been a misused phrase in Christianity, and one I think will cease to be negative if understood in its full context.

Torah is a word which points to the Teachings within the first five books of the Bible. These first five books are what spawned every other Scripture. Without our Greek logic telling us that we are masters of our own truth, we will cling to the Torah as the life preserver we need.

If Jesus is truly the Living Torah as John proclaims him to be, then why do we not embrace the Torah, not because it gives us righteousness but because it contains the truth Jesus was trying to teach us.

Paul explained that righteousness is faith in the Messiah, we cannot be righteous by what we do, but after Jesus makes us righteous we still need to live properly. Within the Torah we can build a proper foundation, rather than building on sinking sand.

Without these five books of teaching there could be no other ones. It just makes sense to study these books how the people who know them the best study them. I do not believe that by studying Torah anyone becomes super Christians, or do I believe Judaism is better than Christianity.

I do believe, without understanding Torah Principles, our life of Discipleship is not as strong as it should be and we short-change our children in respect to a legacy of truth. I know that understanding the Torah better, helps us to be better followers of Jesus. Academic learning is only one part however, heart understanding and doing is the other. To have this true understanding, requires us to know the foundations Jesus took for granted.

Most of the Sages, Torah Scholars, and those who studied the Torah in depth, are from the Tribe of Judah. Now in Israel there is no tribal distinction, the Jews believe mostly, that the lost ten tribes of the Northern Kingdom of Israel are within Israel now. Most Jews do not want to believe there are actual lost tribes who will eventually be returned by God to Israel.

I believe however, this is a key for Gentiles to see as we study the Torah. The Torah was specifically to the Nation of Israel not just one tribe, but all 12 Tribes, it is within this context you study Torah properly.

Some messianic groups say the Torah Commands are for the Gentiles, I think this misses much of the mark. This also misses the Sages teachings about Gentiles. The Gentile Nations rejected the Torah at Mt. Sinai; therefore we will never be able to properly fulfill the commandments because for the most part the commandments are physical commands for someone who lives in Israel, not just ethical ones. The Nation of Israel said they will do, and they will obey, we as Gentiles never said that.

Following Torah did not constitute Salvation when Moses came down with it in his hands, and it does not constitute salvation now. Belief in the Torah (Jesus is the Word of God right), and submitting to the (or His) commands which are for us is what brings salvation.

Jesus made this clear in his admonition to His Disciples, and Paul explained what belief and proclamation does in respect to salvation too (John 14:12-17, 15:5-25, Romans 10:9-10, and Eph. 2:8-9).

In principle, the written Torah contains God's definitions of morality, how to love, how to work, how to act, how to be in this World, but its commands are largely only to the Israelite. This is the sticky part of Studying the Torah. John called Jesus the Living Torah, in the Greek translation it is different but within Hebrew it would be Living Torah.

What does this mean in the context of the Torah? It means as He and the Apostles taught. He embodied Torah in every way, He fulfilled the Torah. God used Him, this Jesus of Nazareth, the Messiah, to create the World.

I have read the Sages teachings about Gentiles; they refer to us as different. It's not a bad or good thing, just different. Our Ancestors chose _not_ to do and obey, as the Tribes of Israel chose _to_ do and obey. I believe I am within Jesus' Nation, which is no Nation to speak of. Jesus never set up an Earthly Kingdom, negating the need to say Believers are a Godly physical Nation.

Nations are of this World, in significance and substance. Our Kingdom will be revealed in the World to Come. To try and make Gentiles more than they are, I think is to run the risk of what has happened to the Church. The Church felt it was in a place it didn't occupy; therefore it strove to fulfill that place, but became prideful, which bred false elitism, and not Unity. To be unified we need as regular believers to look at how we follow because it is the focal point of the coming storm of unbelief which will hit our children.

With Israel being a country again, the Lost Tribes are one by one going home to Israel; no matter what some Jews believe they will see God fulfill His Promises. When all the

Lost Tribes are in Israel we will be looking at a whole different World. Once the 12 Tribes are brought back to Israel, true Spirituality will change most people's Worldview dramatically, it has already started in part.

Most of the Churches pillars or foundations lie in the fact that they have replaced Israel, when Israel has been returned by God to their rightful place, and begin to be blessed by God most peoples 'faith' will wax cold, because most of people's 'faith' is in the wrong things.

We are Jesus' Body, we do not have to be Israel to be loved or special, we already are loved and have a place here. As believers we need to use this time to impress on our Children the truth of whom Jesus is, and why the Scriptures are the only anchor in life. If we do not do this then we will be lost.

There are now three Tribes in Israel that have been ratified as real tribes; these are the Tribe of Judah, Manasseh, and Dan. The Creation of Israel was the most important event of the past Century. We see the influence the Nation of Israel has in a variety of ways, but most importantly for us as believers it is in our understanding of what is true and what isn't.

The Torah is now becoming opened in ways not seen since the days of the Apostles. We are living in amazing times, I believe we need to recognize these things, and stand on the proper side. Society is changing and things we always knew were true, are being replaced by what we thought were not true.

In the Greek logical construct if you do not change your philosophy to line up with the core science empirical evidence, then you are eliminated from Society. Now, because of our stance on Homosexuality, the Church is being eliminated from societal life.

Things like marriage, family life; and the definition of morality itself is being changed because people now believe that homosexual behavior is who a person is, not what they choose to be.

The 1<sup>st</sup> Century Church had a Sanhedrin-like discussion that was centered on whether or not the Gentiles needed to become circumcised in order to follow Jesus as Messiah (Acts 15:1-30).

These types of decrees need to happen again, I pray as believers we can go back to this method that Jesus and His Apostles introduced and get rid of this Greek Linear way of dealing with life.

We do not have to make wholesale changes; we just need to interpret the Scriptures as Jesus did. I think these next 10-20 years will be crucial for believers to see where the church will stand on this. Will we go with Greek thinking and change to fit the science norms of the coming age of unbelief, or will we go back to who we are as followers of a Judaic minded Messiah?

www.ingramcontent.com/pod-product-compliance
Lightning Source LLC
Chambersburg PA
CBHW060155070426
42447CB00033B/1390